COVID-19 and Post COVID-19 Indian Diplomacy

COVID-19 and Post COVID-19 Indian Diplomacy

Vivek Mishra

KW Publishers Pvt Ltd
New Delhi

Copyright © 2022 H.P. Ghosh Research Centre

All rights reserved. No part of this publication may be reproduced, stored in a retrieval system, or transmitted in any form or by any means, electronic, mechanical, photocopying, recording or otherwise, without the prior written permission of the copyright owner.

ISBN 978-93-91490-74-4 Paperback
ISBN 978-93-91490-75-1 ebook

Published in India by Kalpana Shukla

KW Publishers Pvt Ltd
4676/21, First Floor, Ansari Road
Daryaganj, New Delhi 110002
Phone: +91 11 43528107
Marketing: kw@kwpub.in
Editorial: production@kwpub.in
Website: www.kwpub.in

The content of this book is the sole expression and opinion of its authors, and not of the publishers. The publishers in no manner is liable for any opinion or views expressed by the author. While best efforts have been made in preparing the book, the publishers makes no representations or warranties of any kind and assumes no liabilities of any kind with respect to the accuracy or completeness of the content and specifically disclaims any implied warranties of merchantability or fitness of use of a particular purpose.

  The publisher believes that the contents of this book do not violate any existing copyright/intellectual property of others in any manner whatsoever. However, in case any source has not been duly attributed, the publisher may be notified in writing for necessary action.

Contents

Preface	vii
Acknowledgements	ix
Introduction	xi

1.	India's Response: From Regional to Global	1
2.	COVID-19 & Geopolitics: India's Regional and Global Engagements	8
3.	Preparing for a New Diplomacy: Initial Challenges	20
4.	Preparing for a New Diplomacy: Tying Domestic to International	34
5.	Double Whammy: Managing Chinese Belligerence during COVID-19	57

Preface

This monograph intends to map and assess the nature of challenges for the Indian diplomacy during various phases of the pandemic; at the altar of the COVID-19 crisis, during the crisis even as the challenges increased multi fold due to the ravaging second wave of the pandemic, and finally when the country was preparing for the third wave. The changing domestic and international scenarios apropos economic situation, as well as geopolitics, have necessitated significant changes in state behaviour and in the conduct of diplomacy itself. The good old ways of personal diplomacy took a back seat amidst states closing their borders and travel to other countries coming to a virtual halt. The virtual aspect of diplomacy came to be attached as a new normal.

Acknowledgements

This book is a part of research undertaken for the Haripada Ghosh Research Centre in Kolkata. I thank the organisation for supporting this very important project during the pandemic. I thank the Director of this Project, Professor Suranjan Das, Vice Chancellor, Jadavpur University for his constant support and guidance in helping me complete this project, and above all, I thank him for his patience with me as the project was delayed due to several reasons. I also thank Professor Dhrubajyoti Chattopadhyay for his constant support during the project. I must thank the two Research Associates, Dr. Aparaajita Pandey of Amity University and Mr. Fayaz Ali of Delhi University for their very able and sharp support in helping me through research and compilation of documents for this project. Without their help, this project would not be successful.

Completing this project was one of the biggest challenges I have faced, as the evolving situation of COVID-19 rendered severe unpredictability to India's diplomacy in the region and at the global level. In so far as this book narrates the story of India's diplomatic struggle and evolution of its foreign policy since the pandemic began, it remains an unfinished story.

Finally, I thank one and all who were a part of this work directly or indirectly, especially my wife Dr. Tarushikha Savesh whose patience and perspectives helped me complete this work and opened new vistas of analyses.

Introduction

Indian diplomacy faced a *sue generis* challenge during the COVID-19 crisis in many aspects. The population of the country, the number of Indian diaspora living outside India, the informal nature of work force and health infrastructure that in many respects resembles that of developing economies posed unprecedented challenges.

This monograph assesses the COVID-19 and post COVID-19 diplomacy in India by taking a comparative approach. The framework for the draft undertakes two instances of diplomatic relations emerging out of crisis situations. First, the 'Tsunami Core Group cooperation' which was formed in the wake of 2004 Indian Ocean Tsunami and Second, the Vaccine *Maitri* diplomacy which was adopted in early 2021 due to the Covid situation. Although, the pandemic still persists and it is difficult to determine the impact of policies directed towards resolving crisis situations yet an analysis of recent turn of events with the post-2004 diplomatic nomenclature imploring new terms in international politics will be crucial to this study, thus reflecting on Indian diplomacy and its evolution during the various phases of COVID-19.

The first part of the monograph situates India's diplomatic relations in a historical standpoint and what has been the nature of foreign policy since the 2014 NDA government till the Covid times. The focus of this section has been on the 'Neighbourhood First Policy' and draws on examples from various events like SAARC, BIMSTEC, BRICS and ASEAN summits as well as international events. While the second section of the monograph; the starting of the year 2021, focuses on the direct implication of the new forms of diplomacy like Vaccine Maitri which corresponds to Vaccine Diplomacy as seen in the case of China and Russia, more importantly. India has been donating supplies of the AstraZeneca/Oxford jabs produced in the country to regional neighbours including Bangladesh, Myanmar and Nepal, bolstering not only its reputation as a supplier of cheap and accessible vaccines to the global south, but also challenging China's efforts at regional dominance at a time of heightened tensions between the two countries. Whereas Prime Minister Modi has been influential in strengthening diplomatic ties utilising the extents of Vaccine Diplomacy, the book also calls for a look at the foreign policy in terms of the personality of the leadership in enhancing soft power. The comparative assessment of the 2004 Tsunami situation with the COVID-19 crisis presents similar yet different stories of shifts and adaptabiltiy in foreign policy and diplomatic tactics for India.

In the second part, this monograph takes a look at the steps that contributed to both adaptions and evolutions in the patterns of Indian diplomacy, primarily induced by COVID-19 circumstances to cope with the rising challenges in the present times. The 2004 Tsunami in the Indian Ocean and India's response to it can be considered a beginning for Indian diplomacy that took initiative during times of crisis and based itself on pioneering HA/DR operations. India also began to examine the greater geopolitical implications of such initiatives in the region. While the regional politics and its ramifications are easier to observe in the present times, these implications were still a concern in 2004 and a long term strategy to ensure the supremacy for the national interests of the nation have necessitated Indian diplomacy to adopt certain ways of functioning which are critical to a resilient foreign policy. Some of these are examined in this monograph.

Situating Indian Diplomacy in South Asia

India is the largest country in South Asia, having two-thirds of land, population and natural resources. It was evident ever since the decolonisation of the Indian Sub-continent, that India's neighbourhood policy should be of cooperation and for mutual economic well-being. Instead of viewing the security dilemma in South Asia as conflicting in nature and defining their interests in self-help terms, efforts were made to create a social structure in which states trust one another to resolve disputes without war. The Gujral Doctrine in the late 1990s was a similar response towards a new initiative after decades of political unrest, 'offering a series of unilateral concessions to its neighbours without any expectation'. Even the post-2014 government operated on the same doctrine, postulating for possibilities that there might be new avenues to better ties and form new economic alliances.[1]

In its two terms, the NDA government with Prime Minister Modi leading the foreign diplomacy with his famous visits to India's neighbouring regions gained enough international capital to make radical proposals for reforming events like SAARC 2014. This also set a new precedent in following diplomatic ties, 'For instance, under Dr. Manmohan Singh, the coalition government at the centre due to domestic political pressure from the opposition could not make full use of its capacity to transform its relations with South Asian neighbours. With respect to the actions taken by the present till now, it is evident that he understands the importance of complementing both political relations and economic initiatives. Hence, he has made conscious efforts to build and maintain personal contacts with SAARC leaders.'[2] The rhetoric of economic corporation and linking neighbourhood was soon replaced by incorporating new plans like Sub-SAARC networks which proposed to leave out some members of the SAARC nation for amending projects.³ While towards the East, by investing in the BIMSTEC nations India is hoping, amongst other things, to lessen the influence of China in expanding its economic projects.

While in the Covid and post-Covid times, the same translated into health and vaccine diplomacy with equal importance being laid on developing neighbourhood ties. Yet it seems important to locate the juncture between India's earlier diplomacy in dealing with neighbourhoods and how disaster situations like the COVID-19 pandemic influenced policymaking. India's reputation as the 'Pharmacy of world' can surely present itself as an added advantage, when the world order is moving towards a new health diplomacy with a perennial virus threat hanging over the world.

Neighbourhood First Policy and the New Paradigm of Diplomacy

India's Neighbourhood policy before the COVID-19 pandemic and in the days leading up to March 2020 was marked by an attempt by India to better its relations with its neighbouring countries. Developments vis-à-vis Pakistan, Nepal, Bangladesh and Myanmar were pointers in this direction. Exchanges, visits and communications between these countries were witnessing ascendance. India's efforts were mostly centred on Prime Minister Narendra Modi and his various visits to South Asian countries in the earlier days of the NDA government. Starting his tenure in 2014, Narendra Modi invited all the SAARC members to his oath-taking ceremony. This marked an important step in solidifying India's relation with its neighbouring countries.

Further, it continued with frequent visits to various countries starting from Bhutan which PM Narendra Modi said that he had a special connection with India and the relation was termed as 'Bharat to Bhutan' (B2B) Vision.[4] Modi's visit to Nepal was also considered a landmark since it was the first bilateral visit in 17 years by an Indian Prime Minister to Nepal.[5] PM Modi's visit to Bangladesh with the Chief Minister of West Bengal Mamta Banerjee led to the improvement of much-demanded projects like Bhutan-Bangladesh-India-Nepal (BBIN) motor vehicles agreement.[6] Similarly, Modi was also the first Prime Minister to visit Sri Lanka in 28 years after Rajiv Gandhi to take a tour of the nation.[7] In his Afghanistan visit, Modi assured that there will be cooperation instead of competition between the two nations and will progress towards ensuring government to government assistance.[8] India and Maldives entered into a defence cooperation action plan in 2016[9] while the visit by PM Modi to the Maldives was cancelled in the wake of political turmoil.[10]

Along with interacting with neighbouring regions, events like BIMSTEC, SAARC and BRIC were also central to enhance foreign diplomacy. From chairing the 2016 BRIC summit in Goa[11] to inviting the BIMSTEC members for his second oath-taking ceremony, Modi's steps are seen clearly as transforming the Neighborhood policy and promoting economic ties and making inroads in its neighbouring nations.[12] And in the 18th SAARC summit in Kathmandu, PM Modi openly talked about the economic corporation and wellbeing of neighbourhood. The Heads of State present at the summit expressed their strong determination to deepen regional integration for peace, stability and prosperity in South Asia by enhancing cooperation in trade, energy, security, infrastructure, connectivity and culture; and implementing projects in a prioritized, result-oriented and time-bound manner.[13]

But the big challenge in contributing into the politics of South Asia comes from China, where the world's second biggest economy presents India with a possible threat of influencing its partners. Whereas the need for funds by the South Asian countries is largely tapped by China, investing in an initiative like 2015 'One Belt, One Road' initiative and its growing trade with SAARC nation, makes them dependable on China for heavy investments. In 2014 China agreed to invest $20 billion over a five-year period in India. While for Pakistan, the following year China declared an investment amount of $46-billion for the China-Pakistan Economic Corridor (CPEC). Similarly, China had also invested in countries like Sri Lanka, Maldives, Bangladesh and Afghanistan understanding their geopolitical role and infrastructural capacities.[14]

With the Covid pandemic lurking around the globe, the Chinese government was quick to realise the potential of an international diplomacy and to promote confidence in their partner nations especially relating to the BRI project. "Some of the countries in South Asia also received Chinese military medical teams to fight the COVID-19 pandemic, namely Pakistan, Myanmar and Laos."[15] While the Chinese government is using its Covid diplomacy to mend its ill ties in the Southeastern regions, it seems also important how India performs concerning its ties with counties like Sri Lanka, Nepal and Bangladesh. The collective regional response initiated with SAARC nations is already reflecting well, and India making an initial offer of US$ 10 million in combating pandemic crisis sent a strong response in committing towards Neighbourhood first policy.[16]

In the wake of such diplomacy; dictating new norms of international relations, which are being played around in terms of health diplomacy, it definitely corresponds to a much larger challenge for India to compete on both regional and international grounds.

Developing a Vaccine Diplomacy

The history of Health Diplomacy is not new to the western world and it dates to the 14th century 'when early concepts of quarantine were introduced in Dubrovnik on the Adriatic Coast of Croatia' … whereas Health Diplomacy corresponds to Vaccine Diplomacy which 'refers to almost any aspect of global health diplomacy that relies on the use or delivery of vaccines and encompasses the important work of the GAVI Alliance, as well as elements of the WHO, the Gates Foundation, and other important international organisations. Central to vaccine diplomacy is its potential as a humanitarian intervention and its proven role in mediating cessation of hostilities and even cease-fires during vaccination campaigns'.[17] One interesting aspect of post-Covid Vaccine Diplomacy was that it moved from West to East and countries like China became an important player in determining the pace of diplomacy. India, similarly, was also an important participant in responding to the global need for marking strong health diplomacy. Vaccine Diplomacy thus discussed is mostly contrasted in relation to India's neighbouring regions, especially China.

At the beginning of the year 2021, Vaccine Diplomacy also began to emerge as a major theme in international politics. Despite various initiatives like COVAX[18] to ensure global equitable access to vaccine, countries like Russia and China were able to set the precedent for establishing international diplomatic ties with the help of vaccine diplomacy.[19] India was quick too in recognising this opportunity and responding to the situation, especially towards the South-East Asia where China was equally interested in strengthening its diplomatic ties.

India under its "Vaccine Maitri" initiative started sending gift Covid Vaccines to its neighbouring countries. At a relatively early stage of the pandemic countries like Bahrain (1 lakh), Oman (1 lakh), Afghanistan (5 lakh), Barbados (1 lakh), Bangladesh (20 lakh), Myanmar (17 lakh), Nepal (10 lakh), Bhutan (1.5 lakh), Maldives (1 lakh), Mauritius (1 lakh), Seychelles (50000), Sri Lanka (5 lakh), and Dominica (70000) had received COVID-19 vaccines from India as a part of the "Vaccine Maitri" initiative. The commercial supply vaccine had been sent to countries like Brazil (20 lakh), Egypt (50000), Algeria (50000), South Africa (10 lakh), Kuwait (2 lakh) and UAE (2 lakh), Morocco (60 lakh), Bangladesh (50 lakh), and Myanmar (20 lakh).

Towards South East Asia, China's presence has been a constant challenge for India. Events like supplying Cambodia with 1 lakh vaccines and Brazil replacing its demand priority of vaccines from China to India is definitely reflected in good favour. Whereas through vaccine diplomacy, India tried to strengthen bonds with its neighbouring countries while also keeping in check the greater threat of losing its competitive edge on neighbours to China. Countries like Nepal, Bangladesh, the Maldives and Mauritius were important contact points for India to respond to in such times. The Vaccine Diplomacy factor does provide India with a window to expand its influence on its neighbours especially in the Indian Ocean countries where India's influence can match up with China's ambition to translate its Health Silk Road initiative into international soft power relations.[20]

An important diplomatic tie was also established with the Maldives, which received the earliest doses of COVID-19 Vaccine from India. The Maldives has also been an active recipient of India's help during various crises and in 2014 Operation Neer was launched to supply drinking water to the Maldives. In one of his visits to Male, the Maldives, India's Minister of External Affairs also endorsed Maldives

Foreign Minister Abdula Shahid for the candidature of the UNGA President. He said, "In this context, I reiterate today India's strong support to the candidature of Foreign Minster Abdulla Shahid for President of the 76th session of the UN General Assembly next year. Foreign Minister Shahid, with his vast diplomatic experience and his leadership qualities, is, in our view, the best equipped to preside over the General Assembly of 193 nations of the world. We will work together to make this a reality. We would really like to work with you during our membership of the United Nations Security Council for 2021-22."[21] So far as China is concerned, the recent developments strengthening confidence in leadership is a positive set for India to ascertain its position in the Indian Ocean.

India is now the largest producer of vaccines in the world with 60 per cent of the global share, where it has the potential to attract diplomatic well-being and set norms in corporation and mutual assistance.[22] Coupled with policies like Think West and Act East, the possibilities for establishing the road into neighbouring nations will be important upcoming task. It is also important to make sure that local economy set pace with the global order, for economies like China are already recovering. Yet it seems that bilateral and multilateral relation-building could only be the possible way out of the larger pandemic crisis. Whereas South Asia struggles to wake up from the effect of the pandemic in every sphere of life, instance of bilateral relation building is already setting precedent for moving into this new era of Vaccine Nationalism.[23]

Notes

1. *India's Neighbourhood Policy through the Decades*, Ashok Malik, at https://www.orfonline.org/wp-content/uploads/2016/03/GP-ORF_Indias-Neighbourhood1.pdf
2. https://jgu.edu.in/jsia/wp-content/uploads/2019/03/angana-das.pdf

3. *India's Neighbourhood Policy through the Decades*, Ashok Malik, at https://www.orfonline.org/wp-content/uploads/2016/03/GP-ORF_Indias-Neighbourhood1.pdf, p. 19.
4. https://www.orfonline.org/expert-speak/making-modi-bharat-bhutan-vision-work/
5. https://thediplomat.com/2014/08/narendra-modi-to-visit-nepal/
6. http://www.thehindubusinessline.com/economy/india-bangladeshagree-on-power-tariff-await-nod-to-start-supplies/article8093174.ece
7. https://www.nytimes.com/2015/03/15/world/modi-visits-tamils-cultural-heart-in-tour-of-sri-lanka.html
8. https://www.mea.gov.in/in-focus-article.htm?26276/The+Afghanistan+Visit++Highlights+of+Prime+Ministers+visit+to+Afghanistan
9. https://mea.gov.in/bilateral-documents.htm?dtl/26619/List+of+Agreements MoUs+signed+during+the+visit+of+President+of+Maldives+to+India+April+11+2016
10. https://indianexpress.com/article/india/india-news-india/india-maldives-sign-six-pacts-resolve-to-expand-defence-cooperation/
11. https://www.mea.gov.in/bilateral-documents.htm?dtl/27491/Goa+Declaration+at+8th+BRICS+Summit
12. https://www.orfonline.org/expert-speak/pm-modi-new-year-outreach-neighbours-what-means-60653/
13. *India's Neighbourhood Policy through the Decades*, Ashok Malik, at https://www.orfonline.org/wp-content/uploads/2016/03/GP-ORF_Indias-Neighbourhood1.pdf
14. *China's Role in South Asia: An Indian Perspective*, T.C.A. Rangachari, at https://www.orfonline.org/wp-content/uploads/2016/03/GP-ORF_Indias-Neighbourhood1.pdf
15. https://www.orfonline.org/expert-speak/covid-diplomacy-regional-dynamics-southern-asia-65446/
16. https://www.mea.gov.in/press-releases.htm?dtl/32539/PM+interacts+with+SAARC+leaders+to+combat+COVID19+in+the+region
17. https://journals.plos.org/plosntds/article?id=10.1371/journal.pntd.0002808#pntd.0002808-Michaud1
18. https://www.who.int/initiatives/act-accelerator/covax
19. https://www.theguardian.com/world/2021/feb/19/coronavirus-vaccine-diplomacy-west-falling-behind-russia-china-race-influence
20. https://foreignpolicy.com/2021/01/22/india-world-pharmacy-vaccine-diplomacy-compete-china/

21. https://www.mea.gov.in/Speeches-Statements.htm?dtl/33554/remarks+by+external+affairs+minister+at+the+joint+conference+with+minister+of+foreign+affairs+of+maldives+in+male
22. https://www.mea.gov.in/Speeches-Statements.htm?dtl/33558/foreign+secretarys+lecture+on+expectations+from+india+in+the+emerging+world+order+post+covid19+haryana+institute+of+public+administration
23. https://www.orfonline.org/expert-speak/covid-diplomacy-regional-dynamics-southern-asia-65446/

CHAPTER 1

India's Response: From Regional to Global

India has had mixed results in its response to the spread of the novel Coronavirus. While early steps were in Lockdowns, social isolation, and distancing have been a common feature across the world however, as the year of the pandemic progresses, a pattern emerged between India, its immediate neighbours and also the rest of the world. The Indian diplomatic response to the pandemic has been that of cooperation and collaboration. Beginning with the supply of hydroxychloroquine, masks and PPE kits to countries in need to the ensuring ample supply of the Covid vccines, which has now popularly been termed as the Vaccine Maitreyi.

However, it is important to note that the nature of the Indian diplomatic response to the global pandemic is not an occurrence in isolation. A response that bases itself on assuming leadership during crises and building stronger bonds within the neighbourhood and with other countries who potentially could be partners during disastrous situations has been the Indian path towards combating a crisis. It can be traced back to the Tsunami that hit the Indian Ocean on the 26 December 2004. The earthquake that caused the Tsunami had an epicentre near the Indonesian archipelago. It caused widespread destruction and devastation not only to Indonesia but to another eleven littoral countries of the region, with India being one of them. However, despite the massive destruction and loss of life that was faced by India at that time, it assumed the role of the leader and became a front runner in the humanitarian assistance/disaster relief (HA/DR) operations in the Indian Ocean.

The fact that tsunamis are generally quite a rare phenomenon in the Indian Ocean led to a situation where most nations were unprepared for such a natural phenomenon and the aftermath of this disaster. The same was the case with India at that time; however, within a few hours of the Tsunami crashing on the shores of Tamil Nadu, the Indian response was that of leading the disaster relief operations not just for the states that had been hit by the waves but also for the neighbouring nations.

The decision to lead the largest relief operation of its kind in the region did reiterate the Indian vision for itself in the region as that of a regional leader. The disaster relief operations were geared towards the immediate neighbours in the first phase and quickly expanding the radius of such operations. This was bolstered by simultaneous humanitarian assistance in the form of medical teams including doctors, nurses, and emergency workers as well as the supply of essential medicines to stop the potential spread of epidemics.

The operations involved not only disaster relief workers and volunteers but also the navy and the air force for quick transportation and reach. The first wave of relief operations focused not only on the Indian coasts but also went to Sri Lanka, Indonesia, and the Maldives, all nations of the Indian ocean that India has had long-standing diplomatic ties with; the disaster relief operations were conducted with the help of no less than ten warships, patrol boats, and hospital ships. These were further supported by transport aircrafts and helicopters that were filled with medical supplies, relief and medical equipment, medicines, food and water packets, and shelter supplies. As these reached the shores of the affected countries, Indian disaster relief workers set up camp and began their HA/DR operations. They were soon joined by relief and volunteer workers from around the world.

However, it is imperative to notice that though volunteers and help were pouring in from around the globe the Indian government at that time had refused to accept any foreign aid. The then Defence Minister, Shri Pranab Mukherjee articulated quite clearly that "India does not need such assistance at this juncture and it will not take money from foreign governments". A distinction was made between aid from foreign countries and that from the World Bank and the International Monetary Fund (IMF); as India was a founding member of the two international entities. The External Affairs Minister (EAM) of that time, Mr Natwar Singh stated that "we deeply appreciate the offers of help (to India) so far we have managed on our own. Our experience in handling natural disasters has enabled us to develop well-defined institutional mechanisms for disaster management at all levels. It would, therefore, be appropriate that international relief is directed where it is most urgently required."

The choice that India made to take on the responsibility of leading these relief operations in the region and at the same time refusing foreign aid, despite having the same amount of experience in dealing with such situations as other affected nations were interpreted by Graham Allison as India operating on the theory of rational choice. The kind of diplomatic strategy that was pursued by India at that time was termed as crisis diplomacy and was seen as a strategic choice which would help India promote its strategic goals in the region as well as further its status as a regional leader, not only in the immediate neighbourhood but also cement its status in the global stage. The strategic aspects that were observed at that time were as follows.

The Indian initiative to lead the rescue operations elevated the Indian status from that of a victim to a proactive leader and swiftly promoted India into becoming a part of the core group of four countries along with the like of the US, Japan, and Australia; all countries that were providing the highest aid. These were also the beginning of what transformed into the quad much later. The core group, however, was disbanded once the United Nations began to coordinate the crisis management efforts by itself.

The fact that India had offered aid to Sri Lanka as early as the evening of 26 December 2004 which was the same day when disaster stuck, even though it was coping with the devastation and chaos in their own territory firmly planted India in the leadership position. At the same time, most analysts saw and believed that it was a conscious decision to build goodwill with neighbours like Sri Lanka with whom New Delhi has had strained and tense relationships at times. The agility and speed with which India took it upon itself to provide aid were also seen as a function of the rivalry between India and Pakistan by some analysts. According to them the presence of Pakistan and the possibility of it assuming the role of the leader definitely sharpened the Indian desire for a quick and decisive response. There was also the issue that at the same time the US had decided to send 1500 marines and an assault ship. India's move signalled the fact that New Delhi is fully capable of "maintaining its arc of influence in the subcontinent."

In the case of Indonesia, India was quick to send over its two Naval Ships; INS Nirupak and INS Khukri. They were sent for medical aid and emergency relief work to Meulaboh (in Aceh province). The INS Nirupak is a 45-bed hospital ship equipped with an operation theatre and three intensive care units, staffed by four surgeons, an anaesthetist, several physicians and paramedical teams.

The INS Khukri has so far distributed more than 35 tons of relief supplies to the victims of the tsunami in the Meulaboh area. This relief gesture would foster the extended neighbourhood policy of India and strengthen its ties with ASEAN.

At a time when the United Nations is debating the expansion of the Security Council in which India hopes for a permanent seat, the signal New Delhi has sent to the international community through its tsunami relief operations is persuasive.

Finally, by rejecting foreign assistance, the Indian government has willingly invited greater scrutiny of its relief efforts. One can, therefore, expect a "better-than-usual response from the bureaucracy." Already, the Indian air force has mounted one of its biggest peacetime operations.

This better than usual response from bureaucracy has been a trend that India has followed since 2004. The HA/DR operations at the time have become the foundation of Indian diplomatic response in times of a crisis and the Indian response to the pandemic should be seen as a continuation of the same trend. The faith of the international community in India in the context of disaster management and immediate response in times of crisis was observed during the pandemic when the U.S. Deputy Secretary of State Stephen Biegun organized a conference call with close allies and partners to discuss the crisis and ways to coordinate their responses. The call featured senior officials from the governments of India, Australia, Japan, South Korea, New Zealand and Vietnam. The participants plan to meet in weekly conference calls.

Most of the populations in these countries were previously or are currently under lockdowns or stay-at-home orders. While the COVID-19 crisis continues to unfold and evolve in unfathomable ways it is important to understand that the US' confidence in the

Indian capabilities for combating the virus and managing the widespread socio-economic effects of the pandemic are based on the past experience of joint disaster relief during December 26, 2004, Indian Ocean tsunami itself. While the operations led by India have already been discussed; India also participated in joint HA/DR operations with the US.

The tsunami that swept through the region on 26th December in 2004 ended up killing more than 200,000 people, mostly in Indonesia, Sri Lanka and Thailand. Nations from around the world responded by providing disaster relief to the affected countries. The US military conducted Operation Unified Assistance to deliver relief and the USNS *Mercy*, which is currently operating off the US West Coast, was among the ships that participated in relief efforts.

The event and the world's response to it including that of India demonstrated the critical importance of diplomatic cooperation and operational coordination, and this was felt not only by India but also by the US and its treaty allies and strategic partners. The US, India, Australia and Japan formed an active coordination group known as the Tsunami Core Group, run by senior diplomats from the four countries.

Fifteen years later, the COVID-19 crisis presents operational differences with the tsunami relief efforts. There is no critical infrastructure damage around which militaries can focus relief efforts. However, there are some similarities at the strategic level. All four governments have considerable stakes in how they address this crisis within their own borders and how they demonstrate leadership in planning their overseas responses. At present, all are summoning the power of their militaries in various ways. At the same time, all four are currently engaged in larger, strategic-level competition with China over the rules and norms in international politics and economy.

Notably, Biegun's conference call did not include a representative from China, the source of the outbreak.

It is too early to tell if we are witnessing the beginning of a "COVID Core Group." While the pandemic advances, we will need to track how diplomatic cooperation develops and to what extent these nations will activate response forces such as militaries for international assistance. Still, a few lessons from the Tsunami Core Group cooperation are relevant to the COVID-19 crisis response.

There are also greater geopolitical implications of India's initiatives in the region. Maintaining supremacy in the Indian Ocean region and being a persistent counter-balance to the growing sphere of Chinese influence is also a part of the Indian diplomatic agenda. Being perceived as a benign leader of the region most certainly is aided by the display of active leadership.

CHAPTER 2

COVID-19 & Geopolitics: India's Regional and Global Engagements*

Extraordinary response to global crises has often irreversibly redefined future courses for nations. Hitherto, overwhelming responses to most global crises have been by Western nations, led by the US, primarily owing to the asymmetric nature of the global balance of power. However, for at least a couple of decades now, these asymmetries are being readjusted due the rise of Asian countries like India and China. The Asian nations have carved larger space in the global power matrix. Resultantly, their responses to global crises have changed significantly over the past two decades, albeit still often reflected only regionally. The ongoing COVID-19 pandemic is one such moment, at which nations of the future will look back to assess countries by their responses to this global crisis. As such, the COVID-19 pandemic is likely to mark an indelible demarcation between two eras. The bygone, in which the western nations dominated responses in the crises-response binary apropos global crises; and the incoming one where Asian nations will.

In the light of the above sentiment, the Indian diplomacy saw historical steeping up through its diplomacy and political engagements throughout the pandemic. In the aftermath of the debilitating waves of the pandemic, India perhaps finds itself on stronger grounds in

---

* Parts of this chapter was published earlier by the ICWA.

matters of aid to other countries. The COVID-19 outbreak has repositioned India at the centre stage in twin ways. First, by way of its rather effective shielding from the global outbreak of the virus, and second, in its ability to respond far and wide through medical or pharma diplomacy. Some of the most outstanding features of India's new brand of diplomacy is that it includes issuing speedy clearances for export of the anti-malarial drug hydroxychloroquine (HCQ) to over 55 countries, and comprises the despatch of teams of Indian military doctors to countries like Nepal, the Maldives and Kuwait.[1] The Indian medical diplomacy has already had various countries show appreciation for India's timely help. The US President Donald Trump lauded PM Modi as 'terrific' in allowing export of HCQs to US and assured that the timely help "will not be forgotten".[2] Many other countries, including Brazil, Israel and Poland have thanked India for its timely help, albeit not just in sending medical supplies.

Starting the second week of April 2020, India began sending consignments of life-saving drugs as gifts to neighbouring countries to help them fight the Coronavirus pandemic. Among countries in India's immediate and extended neighbourhood India sent drugs to Bhutan, Bangladesh, Afghanistan, Nepal, Myanmar, Seychelles, Mauritius and some African countries. Some countries such as Maldives, Seychelles and Mauritius are completely dependent on the Indian industry for its supplies. The Directorate General of Foreign Trade had placed a ban on export of HCQ on April 4. The government lifted the ban later and decided to supply HCQ and paracetamol. India's decision to lift the ban came on the heels of the US president Donald Trump cautioning that if India decided not to supply the medicines to the US, it could attract retaliations. This led to some speculations about the state of US-India relations. However, India's decision to lift the ban has be understood in the context of its own internal assessments of potential domestic demand and existing supplies. India produces more than 70 percent of the world's HCQs.[3] India has already sent 28 lakh HCQ and 13 lakh paracetamol tablets to 32 countries as assistance. In addition, drug supplies are being made to 42 countries on a commercial basis.[4] India's decision to lift the ban on export of medicines carries two other broader contexts. First, at a time when the pandemic itself has shown no respect for borders, providing medical help across states of the world uplifts India's soft power. Secondly, India's timely help to the US should be seen in the context of possible future reassurances from the US 'regarding India's export subsidies to its producers of steel products, pharmaceuticals, chemicals, etc. which was challenged by the US at the WTO as being detrimental to American workers and manufacturers'.[5] Among other potential benefits, India could also be approaching the US for withdrawal of some of the terms of contention between the two sides at the WTO. For instance, a lessening of the US' pressure on the Non-Violations Complaints which the latter intends to bring into force apropos the TRIPS agreement that would permit a member to raise disputes against a fellow member's policies regardless of a violation of the WTO agreement.

The COVID-19 pandemic has proved once again that India's neighbourhood diplomacy is not based on a top-down approach but on an agenda of friendship and altruism. The COVID-19 epidemic proved to be an opportunity for India to also step up its neighbourhood diplomacy. On April 22, India sent 23 tonnes of essential medicines to Nepal to help it fight the coronavirus pandemic. The consignment which was a gift to Nepal from India included 8.25 lakh doses of essential medicines, 3.2 lakh doses of paracetamol and 2.5 lakh doses of HCQ. India's gesture was personally acknowledged with gratitude by the Prime Minister of Nepal K.P. Sharma Oli.[6] India has also sent drugs to Bhutan, Bangladesh, Afghanistan, Nepal, Myanmar, Seychelles, Mauritius and Sri Lanka where a plane with 10 tonnes of medicine was dispatched. India has sent rapid response teams to Afghanistan, Bangladesh, Bhutan, Maldives and Sri Lanka. In Maldives particularly, a 14-member rapid response team was sent to help set up laboratories and a 15 member team comprising health care personnel from the Army was sent to Kuwait. Moreover, the Indian Air force transport fleet was activated at the beginning of April to transport essential equipment and medicines and at least two warships have been kept on standby for quick deployment in India's immediate and extended neighbourhood.[7] These steps are on the back of a SAARC level initiative started by PM Modi to reach out to all regional nations and creating a SAARC fund of $10 million to be used by the organizational members.

Apart from the medical diplomacy, India turned the COVID-19 crisis into an opportunity to reach out to countries far and wide, evacuate its citizens from other countries, facilitate evacuation of citizens of other countries from India and by providing food grains to countries in the midst of the pandemic. For instance, India has assured Kenya that it would make non-commercial assistance comprising medical supplies apart from commercial supplies. The External Affairs Minister S. Jaishankar has reached out to a host of countries assuring them of Indian medical supplies and other assistance which is constantly updated on his Twitter handle. A quick glance at his Twitter handle reveals that he has already had a conversation with a host of countries. Some of these countries are: Mali, Uganda, Comoros, Burkina Faso, Dominican Republic, Seychelles, Jamaica, Marshall Islands, Jordon, Oman, Qatar, UAE, Saudi Arabia, Palestine, Lebanon, Afghanistan, Estonia, Israel, Panama, Peru, Brazil, Russia, Czech Republic and the US. In Eastern

Europe, 90 tons of medical equipment and safety gear was also supplied to Serbia. India's wheat supply to Afghanistan, cooperation with Tehran in evacuating stranded Indians in Iran and a promise to Malaysia to supply anti-malarial drugs to Malaysia putting behind strained relationship that preceded the COVID-19 outbreak have been some of the standouts in India's diplomacy during the epidemic and truly in the spirit of *Vasudhaiva Kutumbakam*. The extensive proactive diplomacy by India reveals that that the India's diplomacy has been led from the front by the Prime Minister in coordination with the External Affairs Minister.

Beyond what has met the eye, the Indian embassies worldwide undertook a vigorous diplomacy to ensure distressed nationals' return home or safety in their present locations. This was done by issuing advisories and putting in place emergency helplines to assure Indian nationals of their safety. In particular, these initiatives were led by Indian embassies in Canada, Greece, Finland and Estonia, Israel, Japan, Vietnam, Bulgaria and North Macedonia, Russia, Cuba, Brazil, Iran and Switzerland.[8] In a much lauded initiative, the Indian Embassy in the UAE provided alternative places for COVID-19 positive cases and took care of expats who did not have access to food and medicines.[9]

The COVID-19 crisis has also catapulted India's evacuation capabilities at the helm. After facilitating a massive evacuation of 28,000 people from 43 countries just before the global halt[10], the Indian government is also planning a major evacuation plan[11] involving the Navy, the Indian Air Force (IAF) and Air India to bring back Indians stranded in West Asia after travel restrictions due to COVID-19 were enforced. In one of the largest return evacuations of foreign citizens, India has facilitated an Air India special flight carrying 314 Israelis back to their country.[12]

India has so far has been fleet-footed in handling the challenges emerging from the pandemic domestically as well as through international diplomacy. Domestically, India acted swiftly to enforce a nation-wide lockdown. Regionally, it has led from the front in reviving SAARC's framework for creating a common fund pool specifically for the COVID-19 outbreak. Besides, it has sent medical teams, assistance and supplies to regional and extra-regional countries like Maldives, Sri Lanka, Nepal, Bangladesh, Bhutan, Kuwait, China, Brazil and the US. India's timely medical assistance to Brazil has pushed other countries of LAC region like Argentina, Chile, Ecuador, El Salvador to reach out to India for help.[13]

Among great powers, India has kept a fine balance between China and the US. If the Indian Foreign Minister spoke with his counterparts in the US, UK and Australia, he equally engaged Russia and China.[14] India's balanced approach between great powers, especially China and the US which are at loggerheads even amidst the pandemic, is further evident by its assistance to and cooperation with both China and the US. While India has provided 15 tonnes of medical supplies to China comprising masks, gloves and other emergency medical equipment, India has cleared export of hydroxychloroquine (HCQ) to the US. Both China and the US are thankful to India for timely help, and have promised to help India in return. The US has appreciated India's decision to provide wheat to Afghanistan during the ongoing crisis.[15] In the immediate aftermath of India's decision to supply HCQ to the US, the US Department of State cleared[16] Indian request to supply 16 MK 54 lightweight torpedoes and ten Harpoon Block II air-launched missiles for its latest maritime patrol aircraft. From China, India will soon be receiving 15 million PPE kits.[17]

China engaged in an early diplomacy with India after the US President Donald Trump labelled the coronavirus as "Chinese

Virus". In a call between External Affairs Minister S. Jaishankar[18] and his Chinese counterpart Wang Yi, despite showing agreement with China that the virus should not be labelled, India has not shied away from mentioning COVID-19 in its official statement marking 45th anniversary of entry into force of the Biological and Toxin Weapons Convention (BWC). The statement calls for institutional strengthening of the Convention as well as the WHO and has asked states parties to the BWC "to recommit themselves to full and effective implementation of the Convention and full compliance with it, in letter and spirit".[19]

However, India's engagement of China is not without its subterranean notions of friction. Officials in the Chinese Embassy of Delhi have come out strongly[20] in criticism of news reports in the Indian media about labelling the virus as "Chinese virus". Besides, they have also criticised India media over media reports endorsing Taiwan's inclusion in the WHO.[21] Calming nerves, the Indian envoy in Beijing, Vikram Misri, has led from the front in advocating cooperation between India and China to develop a vaccine for the virus.[22]

China is likely to closely watch what ensues after the promise of "coordinated effort" by India and the US in the Indo-Pacific domain. S Jaishankar and US Secretary of State Mike Pompeo spoke over phone to discuss a joint strategy by India and the US to respond to the COVID-19 pandemic.[23] This talk had been followed up by India's participation, led by Foreign Secretary Harsh V Shringla, in a telephonic conversation initiated by the US Deputy Secretary of State Stephen Biegun to discuss a common strategy and share best practices between countries of the Indo-Pacific region. The discussion included representatives from Australia, the Republic of Korea, Vietnam, New Zealand, and Japan with a pledge to continue the discussions on a weekly basis.[24] The framework behind this weekly meeting is being called the 'Quad Plus" which also overlaps with the ASEAN+6 model. Although the success of this group is facilitating a regional strategy to deal with the COVID-19 outbreak remains to be seen, China will be keenly watching the developments and discussions between the Indo-Pacific countries. For India, which has been traditionally cautious about its role in the Quad, a more inclusive model like the "Quad Plus" could provide the necessary operational bandwidth in the region to move ahead with its Indo-Pacific vision. Moreover, with the US and its allies like Japan and Australia increasingly targeting China for the outbreak of COVID-19, there is a possibility of India being cornered in the Quad mechanism.[25] As such, the "Quad Plus" framework is likely to suit India's position better in the current situation.

Given China's continued aggression in the maritime domain despite the pandemic, particularly in the South China Sea, India will be keeping a close watch on China's activities in the maritime domain of the Indo-Pacific. Very recently, its deployment of a fleet of underwater drones in the Indian Ocean which collected more than 3,400 observations[26] has made New Delhi more vigilant.

At the global level, the Indian Prime Minister and External Affairs Minister have engaged with their counterparts in over 50 countries over telephone. India has also regularly shared the steps taken to counter the pandemic with the Indo-Pacific countries through a weekly telephonic call. India's engagement with a host of Indo-Pacific countries on a weekly basis is centred around sharing of best practices like vaccine development, cooperation on straitened citizens and on resurrecting the global economy.[27] The Serum Institute of India (SII) is one of the seven global institutions manufacturing the vaccine in partnership with Oxford University. The government has also given the reassurance that India is working with foreign labs to develop Remdesivir, the new COVID-19 hope.[28]

The COVID-19 pandemic has provided India with the spectrum to lead both regionally and globally. A cluster of middle power countries including Japan, Australia, New Zealand, France, Germany and India has emerged to provide strong leadership in times when both China and the US have not been able to provide direction and leadership. India's call for a reform of the WHO in the most recent G20 meeting has found support from other countries including Australia.[29] And its regional leadership has been appreciated globally. The COVID-19 diplomacy establishes India as a reliable and responsible global power. Besides testing its mettle, how India will continue to respond to the ongoing COVID-19 pandemic will perhaps irreversibly change its course as a more dependable nation regionally, and a more capable nation globally.

Notes

1. Roche, E (2020). "Covid-19 outbreak brings India's 'medical diplomacy' to world's notice". *Live Mint*. April 17. Available at: https://www.livemint.com/news/india/covid-19-outbreak-brings-india-s-medical-diplomacy-to-world-s-notice-11587134032403.html (Accessed April 27, 2020).
2. "PM Modi was 'terrific' in allowing export of hydroxychloroquine to US: Donald Trump". *The Economic Times*. April 10. 2020. Available at: https://economictimes.indiatimes.com/news/politics-and-nation/trump-thanks-india-on-hcq-decision-says-will-not-be-forgotten/articleshow/75056752.cms?utm_source=contentofinterest&utm_medium=text&utm_campaign=cppst (Accessed April 27, 2020).
3. Hazarika, Obja B (2020). "India's Drug Diplomacy: Decoding the HCQ Export Decision". April 19, 2020. *Kalinga Institute of Indo-Pacific Studies*. Available at: http://www.kiips.in/research/indias-drug-diplomacy-decoding-the-hcq-export-decision/ (Accessed April 27, 2020)
4. Gupta, S (2020). "How India turned Covid-19 crisis into outsized global outreach exercise". *The Hindustan Times*. April 23. Available at: https://www.hindustantimes.com/india-news/how-indian-turned-covid-19-crisis-into-outsized-global-

outreach-exercise/story-QfyRaVNWCOcPIj2shq56xO.html (Accessed April 27, 2020).
5. See 3.
6. "Covid-19: India Gifts 23 Tonnes of Essential Medicines to Nepal". News 18. April 22, 2020. Available at: https://www.news18.com/news/india/covid-19-india-gifts-23-tonnes-of-essential-medicines-to-nepal-2588385.html (Accessed April 29, 2020).
7. "Warships on standby, IAF transport fleet activated in wake of coronavirus pandemic". *The Economic Times*. April 02, 2020. Available at: https://economictimes.indiatimes.com/news/defence/warships-on-standby-iaf-transport-fleet-activated/articleshow/74937546.cms (Accessed April 29, 2020).
8. "COVID-19: Indian embassies worldwide issue advisories for distressed nationals". *The Economic Times*. March 21, 2020. Available at: https://economictimes.indiatimes.com/news/politics-and-nation/covid-19-indian-embassies-worldwide-issue-advisories-for-distressed-nationals/articleshow/74746309.cms?utm_source=contentofinterest&utm_medium=text&utm_campaign=cppst (Accessed April 29, 2020).
9. Kumar, A (2020). "Coronavirus in UAE: Indian mission to help Covid-19-hit expats move out of shared accommodations". *Khaleej Times*. April 18, 2020. Available at: https://www.khaleejtimes.com/community/indian-mission-working-on-alternative-facility-for-covid-19-positive-expats-in-uae (Accessed April 29, 2020).
10. "India facilitates evacuation of 28,000 from 43 countries". *The Economic Times*. April 13, 2020. Available at: https://economictimes.indiatimes.com/news/politics-and-nation/india-facilitates-evacuation-of-28000-from-43-nations/articleshow/75115349.cms?from=mdr (Accessed April 27, 2020).
11. Peri, D (2020). "Massive evacuation planned from Gulf". *The Hindu*. April 28. Available at: https://www.thehindu.com/news/national/coronavirus-massive-evacuation-planned-from-gulf/article31457514.ece (Accessed April 29, 2020).
12. "Israel Thanks Air India for Rescuing its 314 Stranded Nationals Amid Coronavirus". *News 18*. March 27, 2020. Available at: https://www.news18.com/news/india/israel-thanks-air-india-for-rescuing-its-314-stranded-nationals-amid-coronavirus-2552779.html (Accessed April 29, 2020).
13. Siddiqui, H (2020). "Coronavirus outbreak: LAC region wants India's help – why it's time to translate Vasudev Kutumbakam into action". *Financial Express*. April 14, 2020. Available at: https://www.financialexpress.com/defence/coronavirus-outbreak-lac-region-wants-indias-help-why-its-time-to-translate-vasudev-kutumbakam-into-action/1927936/ (Accessed April 15, 2020).
14. Malhotra, J (2020). "China is feeling the heat over Covid-19—from Japan to Australia. But India's hands are full". The Print. April 14, 2020. Available at:

https://theprint.in/opinion/global-print/china-is-feeling-the-heat-over-covid-19-from-japan-to-australia-but-indias-hands-are-full/401126/ (Accessed April 15, 2020).

15. "US diplomat expresses appreciation for India's wheat assistance to Afghanistan". *ANI*. April 14, 2020. Available at: https://www.aninews.in/news/world/us-diplomat-expresses-appreciation-for-indias-wheat-assistance-to-afghanistan20200414070757/ (Accessed April 14, 2020).

16. "US State Department Clears Lightweight Torpedo, Harpoon Missile Sales to India". *Tribune Content Agency*. April 14, 2020. Available at: https://tribunecontentagency.com/article/us-state-department-clears-lightweight-torpedo-harpoon-missile-sales-to-india/ (Accessed April 15, 2020).

17. Krishnan, A (2020). "India to get 15 million PPE kits from China". *The Hindu*. April 14, 2020. Available at: https://www.thehindu.com/news/national/coronavirus-india-to-get-15-million-ppe-kits-from-china/article31336317.ece (Accessed April 15, 2020).

18. "State Councilor and Foreign Minister Wang Yi Speaks on the Phone with Indian External Affairs Minister Subrahmanyam Jaishankar". *Ministry of Foreign Affairs of People's Republic of China*. March 25, 2020. Available at: https://www.fmprc.gov.cn/mfa_eng/zxxx_662805/t1761106.shtml (Accessed April 11, 2020).

19. "45th Anniversary of entry into force of the Biological and Toxin Weapons Convention (BWC)". *Ministry of External Affairs. Government of India*. March 27, 2020. Available at: https://mea.gov.in/press-releases.htm?dtl/32604/45th_Anniversary_of_entry_into_force_of_the_Biological_and_Toxin_Weapons_Convention_BWC (Accessed April 13, 2020).

20. Rong, J (2020). *Twitter.com*. April 10, 2020. Available at: https://twitter.com/ChinaSpox_India/status/1248559599474499584 (Accessed April 11, 2020).

21. Dikshit, S (2020). "Indian media's reporting on Taiwan has China fuming". *The Tribune*. March 31, 2020. Available at: https://www.tribuneindia.com/news/nation/indian-medias-reporting-on-taiwan-has-china-fuming-63745 (Accessed April 10, 2020).

22. "India, China can cooperate in developing COVID-19 vaccine says diplomat Vikram Misri". Orissa Post. April 08, 2020. Available at: https://www.orissapost.com/india-china-can-cooperate-in-developing-covid-19-vaccine-says-diplomat-vikram-misri/ (Accessed April 11, 2020).

23. "Mike Pompeo and S Jaishankar discuss coordinated approach to Covid-19". *The Times of India*. April 01, 2020. Available at: https://timesofindia.indiatimes.com/india/mike-pompeo-and-s-jaishankar-discuss-coordinated-approach-to-covid-19/articleshow/74937376.cms (Accessed April 10, 2020).

24. "Foreign Secretary's Conference Call with counterparts from Indo-Pacific Countries". *Ministry of External Affairs, Government of India*. March 20, 2020.

Available at: https://mea.gov.in/press-releases.htm?dtl/32592/Foreign+Secretarys+Conference+Call+with+counterparts+from+IndoPacific+Countries (Accessed April 12, 2020).

25. "US, Australia, Japan target China on Covid-19. Should India join or act in self-interest?". *The Print.* April 14, 2020. Available at: https://theprint.in/talk-point/us-australia-japan-target-china-on-covid-19-should-india-join-or-act-in-self-interest/401596/ (Accessed April 15, 2020).

26. Sutton, H I (2020). "China Deployed 12 Underwater Drones In Indian Ocean". *Forbes.* March 22. Available at: https://www.forbes.com/sites/hisutton/2020/03/22/china-deployed-underwater-drones-in-indian-ocean/#643ab9f56693 (Accessed April 15, 2020).

27. "India shares measures with Indo-Pacific region states to combat Covid-19". *The Economic Times.* March 20, 2020. Availbale at: https://economictimes.indiatimes.com/news/defence/india-shares-measures-with-indo-pacific-region-states-to-combat-covid-19/articleshow/74728105.cms (Accessed April 28, 2020).

28. "Govt says India working with foreign labs to develop remdesivir, the new Covid-19 hope". *The Print.* April 23, 2020. Available at: https://theprint.in/diplomacy/govt-says-india-working-with-foreign-labs-to-develop-remdesivir-the-new-covid-19-hope/407753/ (Acceesed April 29, 2020).

29. "Australia supports India's demand for WHO reform after Covid: Envoy-to-be". *The Hindustan Times.* April 24, 2020. Available at: https://www.hindustantimes.com/india-news/australia-supports-india-s-demand-for-who-reform-after-covid-envoy-to-be/story-3uyqqIqQnMzAIsYQI0PYfJ.html (Accessed April 29, 2020).

CHAPTER 3

Preparing for a New Diplomacy: Initial Challenges

Initial Challenges: Coordinating Relief and Evacuations
After the breakout of the coronavirus from China to other countries, lockdowns and travel restrictions were placed in order to curb the spread of the virus. Towards this first challenge, many countries faced problems with citizens stranded abroad as well as foreign nationals preparing to leave for their respective countries. This task was not only an assurance of goodwill towards allied countries in need but also was a testing point for the nations to check their evacuation measures.[1] Previously in the past, India did successfully execute the largest civilian airlift during the Gujral era, which brought fame to Air India when military Air Force was too cumbersome due to waiting for clearance.[2]

The first evacuation was done on February 1, 2020, with 324 passengers landing in Delhi via an Air India flight from China. But the massive evacuation plan came into force with the launch of 'Vande-Bharat Mission' in May 2020 and by the end of the year more than 10 phases of the mission went successfully delivering Indians stranded abroad. The Indian Navy also launched an operation called the 'Operation Samundar Setu' to repatriate Indian citizens from various countries. During this operation, which ran from May-June 2020 around 4000 nationals were evacuated.[3] By July 2020, Air India had lifted more than one lakh passengers across 53 nations and was already being praised for the commendable job in evacuating such a larger number of civilians.[4]

Redressal and reforms

The Vande-Bharat Mission was a huge success for evacuating Indian citizens from overseas and set an example for India's ability to successfully navigate in a crisis situation. The Ministry of External Affairs in August 2020 claimed to have evacuated around 9.5 lakh Indians from foreign countries.[5] But it also brought forth limitations of diplomacy in managing crisis situations, especially with the pandemic, there also followed an economic backlash and social exclusion.

In May 2020, thousands of Indians stranded in the US faced a critical situation when the new regulations were passed by the Indian government suspended visas of foreign nationals and OCI cards as per the then new international travel restrictions. An article in *The Week* magazine reported 'New York-based community leader Prem Bhandari said that the May 5 travel advisory has created multiple painful issues for the OCI card holders in the US and also to Indian citizens who are either on Green Card or H-1B visas and want to travel back home, but cannot leave their kids who are Americans by birth.'[6]

While in the Gulf countries, especially migrant workers, who were unpaid for months due to the ongoing Covid crisis, found themselves unable to travel due to the high air traffic rates. *The Indian Express* reports, 'A senior officer in the Consulate General of India, Dubai, while speaking to *The Indian Express*, said that from Dubai and Abu Dhabi around 1.50 lakh Indians, including Punjabis, have registered with the Indian consulate to return home. The officer said that majority of them were those who did not get salaries for the past over 6 to 9 months and cannot afford return tickets. However, he underlined that only those who have emergencies would be sent back on these special flights, while others will have to wait for normal flights to start.'[7]

Similarly, towards European countries, the mission was also effective in retrieving the most affected people but a major chunk of workers and students felt the burden of high fare price and growing insecurities towards future endeavours. According to a tweet by the High Commission in London on the availability of flights, it suggested that due to the low number of flights, priority was given to the most vulnerable categories like pregnant women, elderly people and people facing medical emergencies.[8]

Similarly, there was another incident when an Air India Flight scheduled for Korea was halted due to entry permissions. A report further commented, 'In spite of knowing this incident related with two Asiana Airlines Flights and its potential consequences or the Air India flight, both Air India and the Indian Embassy failed to extract any kind of concrete or workable information related to the entry permission for Indian passengers in advance and at the same time being well aware of the backlash from Indian community due to complete mismanagement in the ticketing of 1st flight arranged on 6th of June which was to be converted to VBM flight on 7th of June 2020, where few Indians were denied to board the flight after reaching the IGI Airport, New Delhi, despite the fact that they had paid full airfare in advance.'[9]

The initial task of troubleshooting was successfully executed despite the above laid example of conflict. While these instances involve international law and regulations which in the times of Covid were constantly changing and to see that India navigated through these changes and sometimes offered diligent solutions such problems definitely works towards India image abroad.

SWADES: A Local Solution for an International Crisis

While for the homecoming Indians the government did decide to be more creative with their arrival and launched an initiative called SWADES (Skilled Workers Arrival Data Base for Employment Support). The press release states 'With the aim of making the best of our skilled workforce returning to the country due to the ongoing pandemic, the Government of India has launched a new initiative SWADES (Skilled Workers Arrival Database for Employment Support) to conduct a skill mapping exercise of the returning citizens under the Vande Bharat Mission. This is a joint initiative of the Ministry of Skill Development & Entrepreneurship, the Ministry of Civil Aviation and the Ministry of External Affairs which aims to create a database of qualified citizens based on their skill sets and experience to tap into and fulfil the demand of Indian and foreign companies.'[10] The aim of this initiative was to provide work for those working abroad and it gave a flexible range of options to choose from. A *Hindustan Times* report said, "'The SWADES Skill Form (online) was made live on May 30, 2020, and has garnered around 7000 registrations till 3rd June 2020 (2 pm). Amongst the data gathered so far, the top countries from where the citizens are returning are UAE, Oman, Qatar, Kuwait and Saudi Arabia," the statement said. As per the skill mapping, these citizens had been primarily employed in sectors such as oil and gas, construction, tourism and hospitality, automotive and aviation. The data also suggests that the states which have shown highest returning labour are Kerala, Tamil Nadu, Maharashtra, Karnataka and Telangana, said the official statement.'[11]

Though the initiative was advanced in order to tap on the human work forces which were abroad and provide them with a form of livelihood in India, it was not so fast to look beyond this initiative which built on the famous cultural nomenclatures.

'No less than 4,87,303 Indians have asked to be repatriated during the pandemic. Of those who have managed to return, 20,000 have signed a government register for future employment. The scheme—SWADES—piggybacks on the title of a popular Bollywood film on homecoming in which the protagonist, a NASA scientist, returns to his village and builds a mini-hydropower project to electrify it. SWADES, however, in the government's acronym-speak, is Skilled Workers Arrival Database for Employment Support.'

Whereas the Vande-Bharat Mission did gather support for India to gaining a winning position in dealing with evacuation procedures, it also draws equal criticism at home from the civil society in drawing comparisons with the local migrant workers issue.[12] As the collective amnesia of the civil society progressed with the ongoing pandemic, a new form of diplomacy was beginning to emerge. One that would break the traditional forms of politics and refurnish itself in the veil of old diplomacies, India was now moving towards a diplomacy of friendship.

Points of Departure: An Old Diplomacy for a New Pandemic
The year 2020 presented itself as a very hectic year, not just in terms of international politics and a world pandemic lurking around, but also for foreign policy. Initially, the threat posited by the virus remained confined to China and the rest of the world contemplated its effect on the Chinese economy and politics. But gradually with the spread of the virus to the West, a new dialogue began to emerge, that of post-pandemic world order. It involved looking at the possible effects of the pandemic on sectors like economy, trade, local politics and health care.

Diplomacy thus followed similar suit and we saw a rise in concern over tissues, especially in health care which was to become the forbearer of diplomacy in the post-pandemic world. India similarly responded quickly to the growing concerns over the rise in case of COVID-19. Evacuations, relief measures, lockdowns and controlling of essential commodities for the pandemic took priority. Although, the year 2020 was a challenging year for India in terms of medical infrastructure and managing international diplomacy, it also saw a rise of new diplomatic policy which in turn strengthens India's soft power, especially developing ties in the Indo-Pacific region and the West.

In a world dominated by the talks of the US-China prism which became a focal point of international politics in recent years, Covid presented a new opportunity for the middle powers to raise and influence these arenas. 'There is a tendency to approach the impact of COVID-19 on the international order from a US-China prism. Yet, while the disease has adversely impacted all major economies, there seems to be no serious imbalance in the distribution of capabilities. As a result, hasty assumptions about the current world order could lead to erroneous conclusions. While China has indeed emerged as a dominant player in international politics over the last few decades, this has been accompanied by the rise of other regional powers such as India, Japan, Australia, France, Germany and South Korea.'[13] Similarly, Dhruva Jaishankar writing for the ORF in April 2020, also suggested that the pandemic will interfere with key economic and commercial factors and can also result in gaining a wining hand for countries like India. 'While Indian government spending appears low (suggesting room for fiscal stimulus measures), India's low tax base, considerable (albeit manageable) government debt, and low credit rating erode this apparent advantage. Another area of some promise is India's current account deficit; the pandemic offers an opportunity to redress this, both through the falling cost of commodities (especially energy) and the possibility of a manufacturing boost.'[14]

The critical response has been over the Indian government failing to demands of the local needs and challenges arising from actions in Covid times like lockdowns, economic slowdown, migrant crisis etc. which is being tackled by international display of responses to allied nations in terms of Vaccine Diplomacy.

As similar trends in understanding India's foreign policy also shows that the diplomacy aspect became an integral factor to the growing pandemic response all over the world. An article recently published emphasizes India's 'Twin diplomatic objectives: (1) helping to craft a global policy response to the pandemic in order to avoid a major economic catastrophe with potentially serious domestic consequences; and (2) projecting India's image as a responsible regional and global power'.[15] As such, the contribution of India's Vaccine Diplomacy towards policy making as well as image making has been immense. Furthermore, as has been rightly analysed, "This explains why, for instance, India isn't talking about vaccine diplomacy, but "Vaccine Maitri" (vaccine friendship) to describe its program to donate 22 million doses of Covishield—the Indian version of the Astra Zeneca vaccine—to developing countries. China went a step beyond, outright rejecting the "sinister" notion that it would exploit vaccine distribution to strengthen its global influence."

Along with policies like Think West, Act East, the direction of Indian Foreign policies has shifted a lot during the NDA's government and has taken an indecisive and bold turn. As political pundits comment on the implication of India's domestic polity interchanging with International politics, there is also a persistent haziness about dealing with health care issues.[16] Some of the reports during the pandemic showed a light mood in dealing with the health hazard of the pandemic while impacts on economic life was an early intervention (specailly Rajya Sabha dealings on National Commission for Indian System of

Medicine Bill, 2019 and the National Commission for Homoeopathy Bill, 2019 passed in March 2020 also saw a discussion on Covid prevention). Yet the later phase shows an active, perhaps aggressive participation on the part of the Indian Government in tackling and formulating the pandemic on local as well as international platforms.

Meanwhile, the pertinent position of China in influencing India's foreign policy continued to play an important role as the pandemic progressed. And it becomes more evident that the link between foreign policy in post-Covid times has a direct or indirect link with China. Be it in terms of new global alliances or regional relations within South Asia, the effect of Chinese presence is equally felt.

This however isn't a new phenomenon in terms of international power and such diversion of emphasis on China is in fact more contrasted by the pandemic and thus its influence on foreign policy. For instance, Foreign Minister S. Jaishankar's book *The India Way: Strategies for an uncertain world*, famously notes "This is a time to engage America, manage China, cultivate Europe, reassure Russia, bring Japan into play,"[17] The Indian way was much more reflected in the Neighbourhood first policy which played a significant role in the early 2021. Whereas, the emphasis on America was evident throughout the book as a strong ally, relations with Russia was equally positive. What remains persistent was the curious role of China, though commentaries on the book suggest that Jaishankar thought of the relationship as much of a diplomatic nature rather than declaring an open enemy, by pointing at the 'realism' manifested in the Wuhan summit. Yet we see a clear indication of what India's foreign policy would look like if the Covid situation becomes a deterrent factor.

So what will this really mean in terms of foreign policy and its practices? To begin with, it would require advancing national interests by identifying and exploiting opportunities created by global contradictions. Such an India would pay more attention to national security and national integrity.... Making a visible impact on global consciousness would be taking this to the next level. It would encourage a greater contribution to global issues and regional challenges. Humanitarian assistance and disaster response (HADR) is an obvious platform to demonstrate a more forthcoming posture.[18]

Whereas China's response to the whole Covid situation has been a source of criticism ever since the breakout, and at times the Chinese Government also took to radical strategies in tackling global criticism. A report from early 2020 of ORF notes 'To counter the international censure, Beijing adopted a new strategy, referred to by analysts as 'wolf warrior diplomacy', in which it is using all means necessary to control the international narrative about the pandemic, its roots and its future. It is this motive that has driven Beijing's COVID-19-related aid' whereas India through HA/DR responses has been able to better its ties with its neighbours and allies.

This was what was amplified in India's Vaccine Maitri Diplomacy and the clear contention with China also presents a global response which may or may not translate into soft power but the contentions are nonetheless visible to international perceptions.

Changing International Scenario: Important Events in times of Covid

Some of the important events in which India took part or hosted were: BRICS Summit 2020; G-20 Leaders' Summit 2020-2021; South Asian Association for Regional Cooperation (SAARC Summit 2020); and NAM Summit 2020. The initial assessment of India's outlook around these four events broadens our understanding into identifying the interlocutors of foreign policy and international politics during the COVID-19 times. These events in response to the global pandemic took several measures which did produce a considerable impact on India's foreign policy. For instance, the SAARC summit saw a strong response from India, leading projects like COVID-19 Information Exchange Platform (COINEX), foreign currency swap support and activation of the SAARC Food Bank mechanism. The COVID-19 emergency fund was initiated by India and an initial contribution of $10 million was proposed for this fund.[19] The implication of raising the fund from other SAARC nations and India spearheading the responses of COVID-19 situation by developing COINEX like platforms presents us with an interesting case study in itself in terms of foreign policy. While Pakistan's response to the whole SAARC summit and its health ministers attending the SAARC summit similarly provides for a political insight of India's international standpoints.

Lessons for future crisis
Towards the end of the year 2020 and by the start of 2021, the debate around Covid shifted from debates on lockdowns and providing supplies to procuring and distributing vaccines. The domestic politics, of course played a role in various elections which took place but in the international politics as well, Covid diplomacy was taken over by Vaccines distributions and other such facilities. Especially towards January 2021, the phrase 'Neighbourhood policy' was used along with India's distribution of vaccines to its neighbouring regions which was in accordance with the post-2014 neighbourhood policy. Along with its neighbours, 'Brazil, the United States (US) and South Africa and more than 140 other nations also received essential medical supplies from India under Operation Sanjivani'.[20]

But the real challenge for India lay ahead. The first wave was tackled by initiatives like evacuations, lockdowns, government reliefs, international coordination committees, and finally with the arrival of the Vaccine. By this time India was globally being recognized as a Vaccine distributor and in ways, India was equally challenging countries like China and Russia to gain the upper hand. Diplomacy was also getting ahead with praises from the West, Europe, Latin America, Africa and South Asia. And as India become more certain about growing potentialities in helping allies through its Vaccine Maître diplomacy, India was struck by another Covid wave, the second wave.

After the second Covid wave that challenged the Indian medical infrastructure, the Vaccine Maître policy was equally criticized for the rising cases in India. Shahi Tharoor for instance points out that 'In combating the pandemic, it has gone well beyond the routine provision of health care or the supply of generics. To be sure, it is uncertain whether promoting soft power through health-care exports significantly boosts a country's position in the global order,'[21] which seems to raise more questions when thinking about foreign policy and vaccination diplomacy. Vaccine diplomacy has been an accepted term in international lexicon and there is a wider publicity of India's engagement in the process of Vaccine distribution. Along with the publicity also came criticism about not engaging its own population first in the Vaccination drive.

The lack of vaccines was attributed to not only towards India's Vaccine policy but also led to some drastic changes in the diplomacy itself. Foreign Minister S. Jaishankar on many occasions along with other official heads like Ajit Doval was seen controlling the damage the scarcity of vaccine had caused. These measures in return offered a dimension in India's changing diplomacy i.e. moving towards friendship and banking on the rigorous distribution drive which was the turning wheel for India's Vaccine diplomacy. Needless to say that the repercussions would have been equally catastrophic if India wouldn't have chosen a policy like Vaccine Maître, but since it did the effects are certainly comprehensible. However, it is still debatable that to what extent Vaccine Maître was a successful diplomatic remedy? Perhaps an analysis of the second wave presents us with more answers for this pertinent question.

Notes

1. Chaudhary, Dipanjan R (2020). "Indian Embassies undertake herculean task of community outreach". *The Economic Times*. April 22. Available at: https://economictimes.indiatimes.com/news/politics-and-nation/indian-embassies-undertake-herculean-task-of-community-outreach/articleshow/75285784.cms (Accessed on 20/6/2021)
2. Venkataramakrishnan, R. (2014), "The Berlin airlift was remarkable, but the largest civilian evacuation in history is by India" *Scroll.in July 2* Available at 'https://scroll.in/article/668866/the-berlin-airlift-was-remarkable-but-the-largest-civilian-evacuation-in-history-is-by-india' (Accessed on 20/6/2021)
3. Report by Indian Navy published on their website. Link: 'https://www.indiannavy.nic.in/content/indian-navy-completes-%E2%80%9Coperation-samudra-setu%E2%80%9D' (Accessed on 20/6/2021)
4. 'Air India commences fifth phase of Vande Bharat Mission, expected to run 700 flights', *Economic times*, 1 August 2020, Available at 'https://economictimes.indiatimes.com/industry/transportation/airlines-/-aviation/air-india-commences-fifth-phase-of-vande-bharat-mission-expected-to-run-700-flights/articleshow/77300634.cms' (Accessed on 20/6/2021)
5. "Nearly 9.5 lakh Indians return under Vande Bharat Mission: MEA", *Hindustan Times*, 6 August 2020 Available at: 'https://www.hindustantimes.com/india-news/nearly-9-5-lakh-indians-return-under-vande-bharat-mission-mea/story-8MrEitnPhKQaIvR0jc5qCO.html'(Accessed on 20/6/2021)
6. "Vande Bharat is inhuman': H-1B visa holders slam denial of tickets for US-born kids' *theweek*, May 12, 2020 Available at 'https://www.theweek.in/news/world/2020/05/12/vande-bharat-is-inhuman-h-1b-visa-holders-slam-denial-of-tickets-for-us-born-kids.html' (Accessed on 20/6/2021)

7. Chaba, A.A. (2020) "No money, some struggle to find seat on flights from Gulf", *Indian Express, 10 May*, Available at: 'https://indianexpress.com/article/india/no-money-some-struggle-to-find-seat-on-flights-from-gulf-6402443/' (Accessed on 20/6/2021)

8. "Indian students left in lurch as embassies stay mum on travel" *Times of India,* May 10, 2020, Available at: https://timesofindia.indiatimes.com/city/hyderabad/indian-students-left-in-lurch-as-embassies-stay-mum-on-travel/articleshow/75652404.cms' (Accessed on 21/6/2021)

9. "Air India flight to Korea fiasco: an addled diplomacy, a good up airline and stranded Indians" *Asian Community News,* 5 Sep. 2020, Available at: 'https://www.asiancommunitynews.com/air-india-flight-to-korea-fiasco-an-addled-diplomacy-a-goof-up-airline-and-stranded-indians' (Accessed on 21/6/2021)

10. Press release by GOI, Available at: 'https://pib.gov.in/PressReleseDetailm.aspx?PRID=1628976' (Accessed on 21/6/2021)

11. "Govt to conduct skill mapping of citizens returning from overseas" *Hindustan Times,* 3 June, 2020, Available at: 'https://www.hindustantimes.com/education/govt-to-conduct-skill-mapping-of-citizens-returning-from-overseas/story-ydEmrJAM240CfvyPOMHWXK.html' (Accessed on 21/6/2021)

12. Yamunan, S (2020) "Why isn't there a Vande Bharat mission to get India's migrant workers home?" *sroll.in,* May, 14, Available at: 'https://scroll.in/article/961882/why-isnt-there-a-vande-bharat-mission-for-indias-migrant-workers-to-get-home'(Accessed on 21/6/2021)

13. Harsh V. Pant,Paras Ratna (2020) "The corona-led rise of middle powers on the world stage" 5 May, *Live Mint* Available at 'https://www.livemint.com/opinion/online-views/the-corona-led-rise-of-middle-powers-on-the-world-stage-11588696151544.html' (Accessed on 21/6/2021)

14. Jaishankar, D (2020) 'Economic vulnerabilities and power shifts in a post-Covid19 world' *Observer Research Foundation,* April, 18

15. Pradeep Taneja & Azad Singh Bali (2021) India's domestic and foreign policy responses to COVID-19, *The Round Table,* 110: 1, 46-61, DOI: 10.1080/00358533.2021.1875685

16. Ganguly, Sumit. "An Illiberal India?" Journal of Democracy 31, no. 1 (2020): 193-202.

17. S. Jaishankar, 2020, *The India Way: Strategies for an uncertain world* Harper Collins Publishers, India.

18. Ibid., pp. 18-19.

19. Frumen and Kaul (2020) "South Asia shows new spirit of collaboration to fight COVID-19 (Coronavirus) pandemic" *Worldbank.org,* 31, March, Available at: 'https://blogs.worldbank.org/endpovertyinsouthasia/south-asia-shows-

new-spirit-collaboration-fight-covid-19-coronavirus-pandemic' (Accessed on 22/6/2021)
20. "India sends Covishield vaccines to Mauritius, Seychelles, Myanmar" *Hindustan Times,* Jan 22, 2021, Available at: 'https://www.hindustantimes.com/india-news/india-sends-covishield-vaccines-to-mauritius-seychelles-myanmar-101611280448648.html' (Accessed on 22/6/2021)
21. Tharoor, S (2021) "India's Smart Vaccine Diplomacy" *Projectsyndicate.org,* 11 March, Available at: 'https://www.project-syndicate.org/commentary/india-covid19-vaccine-diplomacy-by-shashi-tharoor-2021-03' (Accessed on 22/6/2021)

CHAPTER 4

Preparing for a New Diplomacy: Tying Domestic to International

The Pandemic led to the world becoming more closed and open at the same time. It was a strange response but as the world started to realise that they could no longer depend on global supply chains and started to look inwards for solutions; they also realised that the only way to combat the pandemic was through collective efforts as well as aid and help. Some nations were more forthcoming during this time with aid, whether it was in terms of providing trained medical professionals and much needed medical equipment or later sending vaccines. India has been one of the countries that was forth coming in providing assistance and aid to other countries, beginning from its immediate neighbourhood region and moving outwards.

It is important to note that the spread of the COVID-19 pandemic, has forced the world to turn towards regionalism more than globalisation once more. The same is true for India and its engagement with the neighbourhood during the Pandemic.

The COVID-19 pandemic brough the ineptitude of the public health sector in South Asia in focus. The health sector in the region has needed additional investment and overhauling for some time and it became apparent during this time that the countries of the region were not prepared to deal with a health challenge of such magnitude. According to the Global Health Security Index (GHS), the ranking of the states of the region would be categorised as poor, some were also calculated to be below the global average. For instance, out of a total of 195 countries, India is ranked 57 while the average score is 46.5, and Bhutan 85 (Global Health Index 2019, p. 8). Barring India and Bhutan, other countries are much below the global average of 46.5. Pakistan finds itself ranked 105, Nepal is ranked 111, and Bangladesh is ranked at 113 (Global Health Index 2019, pp. 20-24). The health infrastructure of the region was not equipped to deal with an emergency which was this massive, at the same time the high density of population made relatively simple measures like that of social isolation and quarantine quite difficult to administer and carry through.

The existing health system was put under even more pressure and as everything came to a standstill due to lockdowns and social isolation, the impact on the economy was also felt, specifically in the unorganised and informal sector. The largest number of unskilled and semi-skilled workers are employed by this sector in addition to the daily wage earners. As the economy in South Asia took a hit so did the livelihood of the workers. India also sends a large number of semi-skilled and skilled labour to other countries, and their remittances form a considerable part of GDP and National Income. Due to the COVID-19 pandemic and the closing down of businesses, these remittances have also decreased in scale. A very real of such shortages and sudden loss of livelihood across the region was manifested on Global Hunger Index, where as per the severity scale, the region was categorised as experiencing 'serious level of hunger'. It is clear that the Pandemic has not just had health effects but also socio-economic impact. While the disease does not discriminate among the economic class of people, the long term economic effects have made the under-privileged even more vulnerable. While India has been investing in its social sectors; the same is not replicated throughout South Asia. This lacunae in the region in social spending and health infrastructure has been recognised by India and following the tradition of crises diplomacy, India set out to provide aid to its neighbours.

Such a pioneering spirit for HADR has been acknowledged as a part of India's Outreach Programme. While it has been a part of the Indian diplomatic traditions for a long, it was reiterated by Prime Minister Narendra Modi while he was addressing the UN Economic and Social Council or the ECOSOC. PM Modi said;

> We have always prided ourselves as the first responder in our region—a friend in need. Be it earthquakes, cyclones, or any other natural or human-made crisis, India has responded with speed and solidarity. In our joint fight against COVID, we have extended medical and other assistance to over 150 countries. (Modi 2020)

India has been labelled as the 'Pharmacy of the world' and the COVID-19 pandemics has tested its mettle. The vaccine diplomacy that India has indulged in has only been possible because of the Indian ability to churn out vaccines at a monumental pace. The same has been corroborated by agencies around the world. While this has been especially true during the pandemic, India has been one of the leading manufacturers of vaccines and medicines since late 1990s. Sixty-seven per cent of all medicines produced in India is exported to developing countries. Out of the essential medicines that UNICEF distributes in the developing nations, approximately fifty per cent are manufactured in India. In addition to this 75 to 80 per cent of all medicines distributed by the International Dispensary Association of the IDA in developing countries are also manufactured in India

(Medicine Sans Frontiers 2007). Such capabilities make India an apt candidate for crises diplomacy in general and Vaccine diplomacy in particular.

Early Phase of Covid Diplomacy

As an early reaction to the COVID-19 pandemic, India announced Covid assistance to ninety countries of the world, worth 1 billion USD. (Gupta, 2020) This aid included the delivery of Paracetamol tablets and later Hydroxychloroquine or HCQ tablets when they were considered helpful in relieving Covid symptoms. Since India is also the largest producer of generic medicines, it also helped the receiving countries with the cost of the medicines. According to Sahay (2020). It accounts for sixty-two per cent of the world's demand for vaccines. The Indian penchant for crises diplomacy has also been tied to the ancient philosophy of Vasudeva Kutumbukam which roughly translates to the world being considered one family.

During this time India maintained a steady supply of critical health care equipment, critical medicines, masks, and PPE kits. To maintain this supply India even lifted the previously placed ban on the export of critical medicines in April 2020. Once the ban was lifted the export of fourteen critical life-saving drugs including HCQ and paracetamol began all over the world. In April 2020, the MEA spokesperson, Mr Anurag Srivastav also made a statement to this effect, where he stated that "humanitarian aspects of the pandemic, it has been decided that India would license paracetamol and HCQ in appropriate quantities to all our neighbouring countries who are dependent on our capabilities" (MEA 2020). India also doubled the production of HCQ tablets during that time. While HCQ is an antimalarial drug, it was found to be useful against COVID-19 and was exported to the world along with Paracetamol tablets. Approximately

446 million HCQ tablets and a little above 1.5 billion paracetamol tablets were exported during this time.

The Indian Pharmacy sector has played a vital role in the Indian diplomacy around the COVID-19 pandemic, it also brought in foreign exchange which formed 1.5 per cent of the Indian GDP in 2020 (Pattnaik 2020) The Indian pharmaceutical industry has increased its production manifold to meet the challenge of this pandemic. The logistics of assistance are also challenging in their own right, the vaccines need to be kept at very specific temperatures far below the freezing point. Even with advanced transportation and refrigeration technology, this is difficult to achieve. The shelf life of the COVID-19 vaccine is also quite short. The Indian pharmaceutical industry also had to deal with these additional challenges while making sure they were manufacturing vaccines.

However, India still took the lead in providing essential medical supplies to numerous countries of the world, especially among its immediate neighbours of South Asia, this can be attributed to the spirit of 'neighbourhood first' and the 'first responder to a crisis'. As foreign Secretary Harsh Vardhan Shringla said,

> Health diplomacy is a subset of this larger machinery of multilateral diplomacy ... India's role as a 'pharmacy of the world' has come into focus during this pandemic. We have a world-class pharmaceutical industry that is the producer of choice for critical medications with brand recognition in all geographies and markets ... went out of its way to be a net provider of health security. (Shringhla 2020)

Prior to the outbreak of the COVID-19 pandemic, India was already considered a popular destination for health tourism as it was cheaper than most other places with well qualified medical professionals and well-equipped hospitals. This has been especially true for the people from neighbouring countries, for medical treatment. This reflected the growing footprint of the health sector in attracting tourists and the world-class health care facilities, even though mostly private, at an affordable price. Out of total tourists arriving in India in 2019, 6.4 per cent came for medical treatment in India (Government of India 2020, p. 5). These medicals capabilities gave India the requisite qualification needed to play a leadership role in this situation of the Pandemic.

COVID-19 Assistance in the Neighbourhood

India was prompt in providing assistance around its neighbourhood, a mere four days after the beginning of the first vaccination programme inside the country on January 15, 2021, India sent the first consignment of 150,000 doses of Covid Vaccine to Bhutan. Prime Minister Lotay Tshering was very appreciative of India's help and in his description of the Indian initiative he mentioned, "It is the display of altruism at best" and he also said, "It is of unimaginable value when precious commodities are shared even before meeting your own needs, as opposed to giving out only after you have enough" (Prime Minister's Office 2021). Following a similar pattern, in the first phase itself Bangladesh received 2 million doses of the vaccine, Nepal was sent 1 million doses, 100,000 doses were sent to the Maldives, another 1.5 million doses to Myanmar and 500,000 doses to Sri Lanka. These vaccines were supplied as part of grant-in-aid. External Affairs Minister of India tweeted, 'Putting neighbours first, putting people first!'

According to Mishra (2020), India has already pledged ₹67.8 million worth of aid to Nepal, out of which, aid worth ₹39.3 million has already been delivered. Aid worth ₹39.7 million was pledged to Bangladesh by India, and ₹36.1 million worth of aid has been delivered so far. Afghanistan on the west of India was pledged a total of ₹22.3 million worth of aid, and so far, aid worth only ₹2.9 million has been delivered to the Afghan nation. The first instalment of the emergency medical assistance that was sent to Bangladesh contained 30,000 surgical masks and 15,000 head-caps was sent over on March 25, 2020. The subsequent Indian consignment was made up of 50,000 sterile surgical latex gloves and 100,000 HCQ medicine tablets which reached on the 26th of April 2020. Then on the 6th of May 2020, the third consignment which consisted of 30,000 RT-PCR COVID-19 test kits (AIR 2020) was handed over. It is important to note that India provided essential and continued aid throughout the year as the pandemic progressed. In November 2020, Bangladesh signed a deal with the Serum Institute of India to buy 30 million doses of coronavirus vaccine developed by British drugmaker AstraZeneca.

The Government of Sri Lanka (GoSL) had requested India for aid and assistance with Covid management and in April 2020 India gifted approximately 13 tonnes of essential, life-saving drugs to Sri Lanka. Sri Lanka received several help consignments from India, the second consisted of sterile, surgical, latex gloves—essential for mitigating contamination. The next one constituted of more medicines and gloves, and the fourth consignment consisted of a massive 12.5 tonnes of medicines and medical equipment which was sent by a special Indian flight on May 8, 2020 in Sri Lanka.

India has always shared a special relationship with Nepal and during the pandemic, this was not lost on the two nations. In April 2020, India provided Nepal with a total of 825,000 doses of essential medicines which included 320,000 doses of paracetamol and 250,000 doses of HCQ in addition to test kits and other medical supplies.

In May of 2020, India sent another consignment that consisted of 30,000 PCR kits and 28 Intensive Care Unit (ICU) ventilators to Nepal. During the foreign Secretary's visit to Kathmandu, 2,000 vials of Remdesivir injections were gifted to the country. Since 1994, India has carried on the tradition of providing Nepal with medical aid, since then, India has gifted Nepal 823 ambulances, and in 2021 with the changing demands of the pandemic, India supplied Nepal with all three categories of ambulances; Advance Life Support category, Basic Life Support and Common Life Support ambulances. India has also assured the country that it would supply Nepal with COVID-19 vaccine as assisting neighbours is one of India's top priorities in the region. The Nepalese Prime Minister K. P. Oli was very grateful and thanked India for the generous help by tweeting 'at this critical time when India is rolling out vaccination for its own people'.

Moving ahead with Vaccine diplomacy in the region, India then signed an MoU with the Maldives to establish a Drug-Detox centre with MVR 8 million grant assistance. Since January of 2021, India has been supporting the Maldives to combat the COVID-19 pandemic. India sent a 14-member COVID-19 Rapid Response Team of doctors and specialists to the Maldives and the Indian Air Force provided the country with medicine worth 11.7 tons under operation *Sanjeevani* (MoD, 2020), it also included 580 tons of food aid (HCI, Maldives, 2020, April). In addition to all this India lifted the previously put restrictions on import of medical consumables, respiratory apparatus and testing kits (HCI, Maldives, 2020, September 21). India has also permitted approximately 500 critically ill Maldivian patients to come to India for medical treatment. India supplied Maldives with a total of three consignments of medical supplies, which also included 200,000 HCQ tablets.

India agreed to collaborate with the neighbours of vaccine trails and also to co-produce vaccines itself. India is also utilizing its superior capabilities of health and medical expertise and making it available to the entire South Asian region. (Shringala, 2020)

As a part of the ITEC programme, India has also provided e-training or training via remote learning set up to medical professionals across the South Asian nations under the aegis and in collaboration with the All India Institute of Medical Sciences (AIIMS) and Post Graduate Institute of Medical Education & Research (PGIMER), Chandigarh. AIIMS, Bhubaneswar also conducted the training in the Bangla language so as to assist the participants from Bangladesh. India has also collaborated with its neighbours in the region during the third phase of the vaccine trial, India has trained them to conduct the second and the third phase of the vaccine trials themselves, thereby helping the region become more self-reliant. The first phase of the 6-8 weeks training programme focused on the consolidation of the clinical trial research capacity by building several technical capacities of medical professionals and health care workers in the region. This training programme saw participation by investigators, epidemiologists, clinicians and representatives from Nepal, Maldives, Bangladesh, Mauritius, Sri Lanka, Bhutan and Afghanistan (PIB 2010).

COVID-19 and India's Regional Economic Diplomacy

The chief challenge that presented itself due to the COVID-19 pandemic was the cross-border trade which came to an almost grinding halt once complete lockdowns and stringent measures were announced by all countries of the region. The World Bank has estimated a likely shrinking of the economies of the region in 2020. According to the estimates, the stalling of economic activities would lead to a contraction of the economies of Afghanistan from 3.8 to 5.9 per cent, for Bangladesh, it is 2.0 to 3.0 per cent, India might see a contraction of 4.8 to 5.0 percent, the Maldives is estimated at 8.5 to 13.0 per cent, Nepal 1.5 to 2.8 per cent, Pakistan anywhere from 1.3 to 2.2 per cent and Sri Lanka from 0.5 to 3.0 per cent (World Bank 2020).

Cross-border trade has a proclivity to be labour intensive thereby providing livelihood to a large number of people. The highly contagious nature of the virus resulted in an almost complete shut down of the trade. It is also important to note that most of the items that are traded across these borders are termed as essential items and/or perishable goods. The government promptly announced a 'round-the-clock' clearance of goods at all customs facilities on 20 February 2020. On 24 February, the Chairman of the Department of Revenue issued an instruction asking for a 24×7 mode of functioning of the Custom stations and also asked the officers to show greater sensitivity for the cargoes coming from the affected area and waiving of late fees due to the delay in the receipt of documents thereby helping in the easing of the situation (CBITC February 2020). Shipping lines were also asked to not levy any detention charges on containers. To speed up the process further, machine-based automated release of import consignments was launched throughout India from March 5, 2020. The Union Ministry of Finance on March 24, 2020 informed the major ports of the country that the COVID-19 pandemic should be considered a calamity and that would entitle invocation of 'force majeure' provisions. All major ports during the pandemic had been directed to not levy penalties, demurrage, charges, fee, rental on any port user (traders, shipping lines, concessionaires, licensees, etc.) for any delay in berthing, loading/unloading operations, or evacuation/arrival of cargo caused by reasons attributable to lockdown measures

(Ministry of Shipping March 31, 2020). The same was also directed to the authorities at the airports, inland container depots and container freight stations. While this step would result in India losing a considerable sum in the form of revenue, it was seen as a grand gesture of goodwill.

Post the announcement of the country-wide lockdown in India, as anticipated there was severe congestion at the land border stations, especially in the Petrapole-Benapole border between India and Bangladesh (Bhattacharya April 2020) and Birgunj-Raxaul, Biratnagar-Jogbani, Bhairahawa-Sunauli and Nepalgunj-Rupediya Land custom stations. Nepal being a land-locked country has no ports of its own, and there it also uses the Indian ports of Kolkata, Haldia, Vishakhapatnam and Kandla for its external trade in addition to using Chittagong and Mongla ports in Bangladesh. At the same time its important to note that some of the trading points remained closed, which had an adverse impact on the local businesses. India has followed an open border practice between India and Nepal which has allowed for free movement across the two countries as per the border treaty of 1950, however as states of India also restricted passenger and freight movement due to the spread of COVID-19, it also affected the free flow of people and goods across the two countries.

To assist with the free flow of trade even during Covid and social distancing, India introduced faceless assessment, a technological advancement that would help in the assessment of goods and people with minimum physical contact for import and export purposes (CBITC, June 2020). As Bhutan in addition to Nepal also used Indian ports due to being a land locked country, the trade between the Bangladesh Bhutan India and Nepal (BBIN) countries was also affected as India was the transit nation. Nepal and Bhutan both use India to trade with Bangladesh and vice versa. On April 8, 2020, in a meeting of senior officials who dealt with trade between the SAARC countries, in an effort to ease trade, the members discussed provisional clearance of imports, accepting digitally signed certificates of origin, and scanned copies of documents for clearance of imports customs and release of payments by a bank (MEA April 7, 2020). India's total export to South Asia was US$ 21.9 billion in 2019-2020; however, from April to September 2020 it is US$ 8.0 billion; India's total export was US$ 474.709 million in 2019-2020; however, from April up till September 2020, it stands at US$ 149.534 million, which shows how cross-border trade felt an impact of the COVID-19 pandemics (Government of India 2020).

India's diplomacy in the region also included debt reschedules and currency swaps so as to alleviate the situation the region was already facing and continues to face. For instance, on the 22nd of July 2020, India and Sri Lanka had a technical discussion on the rescheduling of bilateral debt repayment by Sri Lanka. India agreed to a currency swap deal of US$400 million against Sri Lanka's request for a special US$ 1.1 billion. India has also provided budgetary support of US$ 250 million in soft loans to aid the Maldives in overcoming its financial difficulties. The Maldives has an option of payment of this loan after 10 years with a bi-annual interest payment (HCI, Maldives September 21, 2020). The Maldives had also signed a 400 million USD currency swap during President Ibrahim Solih's visit to India in 2019. Maldives has already transferred US$ 150 million in August 2020 and it faces an economic crisis due to the devastation that is being faced by the travel and tourism industry, which is the chief source of foreign exchange for the country, any help in repayment of loans is welcomed by the country.

While such currency swaps have been a part of India's diplomacy in the region, in the times of COVID-19 and economic distress, it provides some much needed relief and helps to the countries of the region. The currency swap is not a Covid phenomenon and it must be noted that even in March 2015 India had extended the option of a currency swap facility to all the members of SAARC. In a press release, the Reserve Bank of India had noted,

> The swap arrangement is intended to provide a backstop line of funding for the SAARC member countries to meet any balance of payments and liquidity crises till longer-term arrangements are made or if there is need for short-term liquidity due to market turbulence. The arrangement will also further financial stability in the region. (Reserve Bank of India, 2015)

India and SAARC COVID-19 Fund

On the 13th of March 2020, Prime Minister Modi said in a tweet, 'I would like to propose that SAARC nations' leadership chalk out a strong strategy to fight Coronavirus' (*The Wire* 2020) The fund was proposed outside the SAARC calendar of routine activities. It has been seen as the most rapid path to act without being held back by the procedural details that the SAARC process involves in regular events, it has been seen as the best possible option (Pattanaik 2020). Ministry of External Affairs, in a statement, said 'India's belief that sharing of resources, expertise, best practices and capacities in these challenging times would go a long way in bringing the countries in the SAARC region closer together' (MEA March 23, 2020).

The India-Pakistan conflict, however, has remained a major obstruction in the SAARC process. The two countries have different ideas about regional cooperation owing to their history of conflict. While India does not particularly need SAARC to conduct trade and have relations with its neighbours, the centrality of India's geographical location does give India an upper hand in conducting bilateral trade with its neighbours, however, India does consider SAARC important to India's regional diplomacy. Perhaps that is the reason why India proposed SAARC COVID-19 Fund. As Prime Minister Narendra Modi said,

> We should evolve common SAARC Pandemic Protocols which can be applied on all our borders as well as within our borders in such situations. This can help to prevent such infections from spreading across our region and allow us to keep our internal movements free. (MEA March 15, 2020)

The initiative was not without obstacles, the conflict with Pakistan does tend to take over most of the Indian issues in the region and the same happened on the 16th of March 2020 when in the SAARC meeting Pakistan chose to talk about Kashmir instead of coherent and collective plan to combat the COVID-19 pandemic. The other nations were, however, more interested in finding solutions to the situation they and the entire world was in and therefore, looked forward to regional initiatives to fight the pandemic. All the countries, except Pakistan, directly made pledges to contribute to the SAARC COVID-19 Fund, which made the pledge of 3 million USD and stated that its contribution would be parked with the SAARC Secretariat to fight COVID-19. This contribution came after all the member-states of the SAARC announced their contribution. This does reflect on the divergence of opinion between India and Pakistan on the ways and means of administering the fund, it is also emblematic of the fact that at times India's regional diplomacy does become a hostage to India-Pakistan bilateral relations.

India contributed US$ 10 million to begin the regional SAARC Fund which went on to constitute 50 per cent of the total fund. Sri Lanka contributed US$ 5 million, this was followed by Bhutan which pledged 100,000 USD, Bangladesh pledged US$ 1.5 million, and finally, Maldives pledged 200,000 USD. Pakistan while contributed a considerable amount of US$ 3 million, it decided to place its contribution with the SAARC Secretariat instead of the fund. The SAARC Development Fund has also committed US$ 5 million under its social charter to fight COVID-19. As mentioned before, India has already sent medical equipment worth US$1 million to Nepal, Bhutan, Bangladesh and Maldives from the contribution it has pledged to the Fund.

The money pledged for the SAARC COVID-19 Fund still remains at the disposal of individual member countries and can be spent at times when a member country requests help from a particular country's dedicated fund. Since the fund remains outside of the SAARC process, the individual member countries would administer it as they wish without getting stuck in the bureaucratic process. Such an approach highlighted the fact that the initiative is focused on the benefit of the region.

India has also introduced the SAARC COVID-19 Information Exchange Platform (COINEX) for the member countries to inspire frequent exchanges so as to help all the countries and finding collective solutions to COVID-19 and its mutations. It has been said that the objective of this platform is to serve as a; a multipurpose platform to further discuss and organise activities such as online training for emergency response personnel, knowledge partnerships, sharing of expertise in disease surveillance, including the corresponding software, and joint research for new diagnostic and therapeutic interventions for epidemic diseases. Within the SAARC framework,

COINEX demonstrates the worth and effectiveness of collective action to deal with common challenges for collective good (SAARC-COINEX 2020a). The SAARC Disaster Management Cell also hosted the SAARC COVID-19 website in Gandhi Nagar in Gujarat and the uniqueness of the website lies in the fact that real-time data is available on the site, which aided Information Exchange Platform (IEP) to help in mutual learning.

From the SAARC COVID-19 Fund, which has been earmarked for the region, India has used US$ 1.7 million to provide drugs, medical supplies and machines to Afghanistan, Bhutan, Bangladesh, Nepal, Maldives and Sri Lanka. The does not include the transportation of the relief commodities, which has, in some sectors, translated into two or even three times the value of the relief material as the aid was provided via chartered flights from New Delhi due to the time sensitive nature of this operation (Gupta 2020a).

However, as prompt and good intentioned the formation of the fund was, after few meetings, the SAARC COVID-19 Fund fell prey to policy paralyses due to India-Pakistan bilateral issues taking centre stage instead of the COVID-19 challenges being brought into focus during the meetings. While it is a proverbial bump in the road for India's regional diplomacy, it can not be considered a failure as India still managed to initiate a fund for the collective welfare of the region. Nevertheless, more creative solutions to circumvent the India-Pakistan problem during the SAARC summits could have been used.

Challenges to Overcome in Taking Forward the Vaccine Maitri

While India's relations with its neighbours is deep-rooted, and mostly amicable they are not without their issues. India as the geographically and economically largest country in the region is often accused of meddling in the internal politics of its neighbouring countries. This is very much evident in India's relations with Nepal, Sri Lanka, and Myanmar which have had their share of ups and downs. However, India's regional policy and also the response of its neighbours being subjected to scrutiny and feeds into domestic politics making both India and its neighbours extremely cautious about their diplomatic initiative. India's vaccine diplomacy ran into trouble when a media report, quoting the Press Trust of India, stated that the Indian army is readying separate teams to boost the capabilities of security forces involved in pandemic duty in the neighbouring countries, especially in Bangladesh, Sri Lanka, Afghanistan, etc. to help them build capacity. The media report of India sending a 15-member Rapid Response Team to the Maldives and Kuwait as part of a bilateral agreement perhaps gave rise to such speculation. This news created an unnecessary disturbance and raised apprehensions about sovereignty. For instance, the Sri Lankan Defence Secretary, Maj Gen Kamal Gunaratne had to clarify to his people that no such discussion had ever taken place and that the Sri Lankan Army was at the forefront of the country's fight against the COVID-19 pandemic. Similarly, the Bangladesh Foreign minister, A. K. Abdul Momen also explained that Bangladesh had not sought any such assistance from India and rather it had despatched its military team to the country of Kuwait. These clarifications thankfully put any further speculations to rest. However, the apprehensions in the region continue for some reason or the other. It is interesting to note that both India and China were at the forefront of mask diplomacy and both play a vital role in the region. However, it is undisputed that India has taken a lead in vaccine diplomacy by producing and distributing Covaxin by Bharat Biotech and Covishield by the Serum Institute of India (SII).

India's private health care sector plays a vital role in its trade, foreign investments, foreign aid, and now in vaccine diplomacy. It also is responsible for the burgeoning medical tourism in India. The vaccine diplomacy in all probability would help in strengthening India's regional diplomacy that is often blemished by doubt and mistrust. India's initiatives in the region often fall prey to a narrative that often projects India as a 'hegemon' in the region. There was also the question of misinformation about the efficacy of vaccines that led to some initial setbacks. However such rumours are also being combated through campaigns to spread accurate information by India through which the government is trying to counterbalance some of the misinformation that has already been spread.

The success of the vaccine diplomacy also depends on the production of an adequate number of doses for the vaccination of India's own citizens who also n need to be inoculated against COVID-19. The obvious concerns of not having enough vaccines for its own citizens has led to some set backs but also an outpouring of help for India from other nations, especially those that initially received aid packages from India.

It is clear that though one could have their misgivings about the Indian Vaccine diplomacy or Maitreya it has cemented India's relations with not just its neighbours but also countries around the world. It was not just a strategic initiative but also a humanitarian one and it has built not only goodwill for India, but it has also managed to play a strategic role in counter balancing the vaccine diplomacy of China as well as bringing together the QUAD group of countries as well as bringing the region closer than before.

It is also important to note that there are certain long term impacts of Vaccine diplomacy for India. The COVID-19 virus has shifted focus to public health as a part of national strategy. Public health has long been considered a topic of proverbially 'soft' politics and yet presently, international public health has become a novel yet integral aspect of international relations between countries. The increased significance of international public health has led to vaccine diplomacy emerging as an effective diplomatic tool for nation-states. As a rising power looking to enhance its role and influence in the international system, India was quick to recognise this opportunity and play its part in international healthcare management. India's leading position as a manufacturing hub of generic drugs and vaccines most definitely provided an advantage over other nations. India is currently the world leader in producing generic medicines, accounting for 20 percent of their global production and 62 percent of global demand for vaccines.

Vaccine diplomacy is essentially a form of public diplomacy. It can be defined as an indirect form of diplomacy that targets the people of other nations more than the governments. It focuses on generating interest and communicating with foreign publics to create a favourable perception, understanding, and goodwill about a country's policies and overall image. Fundamentally anchored in the idea of advancing a country's national interest through attraction rather than coercion, at the core of public diplomacy practice is a people-oriented approach aimed at cultivating and maintaining public goodwill and influencing foreign governments through their publics. The general public is the most immediate beneficiary of vaccine diplomacy, reflecting its advantage for enhancing public opinion and reputation-building in the international arena.

Conclusion

It has been well established that the Indian diplomatic patterns of functioning have involved assuming the leadership role in times of crisis. The Indian penchant for crises diplomacy has earned it goodwill and leadership positions in the past and at the same time played a pivotal role in helping India build and deepen ties around the region and with the rest of the world.

Vaccine diplomacy has helped India take it a step further as India provides its neighbours and the world with much needed assistance and help. It has cemented India's role not only as a leader but also as a dependable ally.

References

Global Health Security Index", Centre for Health Security, Johns Hopkins University (p. 8). https://www.ghsindex.org/wp-content/uploads/2020/04/2019-Global-Health-Security-Index.pdf

Global Hunger Index. (2019). *Global Hunger Index*. https://www.globalhungerindex.org/results.html

Government of India. (2020). *India Tourism Statistics at a Glance—2020*. Department of Tourism, Government of India. https://tourism.gov.in/sites/default/files/2020-09/ITS%20at%20a%20glance_Book%20%282%29.pdf

Government of India. Trade statistics. Ministry of Commerce and Industry, Department of Commerce, Government of India. https://commerce.gov.in/trade-statistics/

Gupta, S. (2020a). India spends $1.7 million from SAARC COVID-19 Fund, Imran Khan is again AWOL. *Hindustan Times*. https://www.msn.com/en-in/news/newsindia/india-spends-dollar17-million-from-saarc-covid-19-fund-imran-khan-is-again-awol/ar-BB12MIqK

Gupta, S. (2020b). India draws up Rs 1 billion COVID-19 medical assistance plan, targets 90 countries. *Hindustan Times*. https://www.hindustantimes.com/india-news/india-amps-up-covid-19-medical-assistance-plan-targets-to-reach-90-countries/story-0X1H8z1Zqi9piw6n4FDu8J.html

HCI, Maldives. (2020). *Press Release*, Budgetary Support of $250 million, https://hci.gov.in/male/?11516?000

High Commission of India (HCI) Maldives (2020). *Press Release on Food aid to Maldives*, https://hci.gov.in/male/?10980?000

Indian Air Force (IAF). (2019). *Aid to Civil Power*, https://indianairforce.nic.in/content/aid-civil-power

Indian Embassy. (2019). *India-Nepal Bilateral Relations*. Kathmandu https://www.indembkathmandu.gov.in/page/about-india-nepal-relations/

Kumar, V. (2013). India well positioned to become a net provider of security: Manmohan Singh. *The Hindu.* http://www.thehindu.com/news/national/india-well-positioned-to-become-a-net-provider-of-security-manmohan-singh/article4742337.ece)

Ministry of External Affairs (MEA). (2020). Video Conference of senior trade officials of SAARC countries on dealing with the impact of COVID-19 on intra-regional trade. https://www.mea.gov.in/pressreleases.htm?dtl/32622/video+conference+of+senior+trade+officials+of+saarc+countries+on+dealing+with+the+impact+of+covid19+on+intraregional+trade

Ministry of External Affairs (MEA). (2020). Official Spokesperson's response to media queries on COVID19 related drugs and pharmaceuticals.https://mea.gov.in/response-to-queries.htm?dtl/32619/Official_Spokespersons_response_to_media_queries_on_COVID19_related_drugs_and_pharmaceuticals

Ministry of External Affairs (MEA). (2020). PM's Remarks on Way Forward at Video Conference of SAARC Leaders on combating COVID-19. https://www.mea.gov.in/Speeches-Statements.htm?dtl/32538/pms+remarks+on+way+forward+at+video+conference+of+saarc+leaders+on+combating+covid19

Ministry of External Affairs (MEA). (2020). Follow up on the Video Conference of SAARC Leaders on COVID-19. https://www.mea.gov.in/press-releases.htm?dtl/32595/Follow_up_on_the_Video_Conference_of_SAARC_Leaders_on_COVID19

Ministry of External Affairs (MEA). (n.d.). Lines of Credit for Development Projects. https://mea.gov.in/Lines-of-Credit-for-Development-Projects.htm

Medicine Sans Frontiers. (2007). Examples of the importance of India as the "Pharmacy of the Developing World". https://msfaccess.org/examples-importance-india-pharmacy-developing-world

Ministry of Defence (MoD). (2020). IAF Continues Its Support Towards Fight Against Coronavirus (COVID-19). *Press Information Bureau.* https://pib.gov.in/PressReleasePage.aspx?PRID=1610800

Ministry of Shipping. (2020, March 31). Government of India https://rai.net.in/Advocacy_Files/26-03-2020/Ministry-of-shipping.pdf

Mishra, S. (2020). China among largest recipients of India's COVID aid, reveals RTI reply. *The Week.* https://www.theweek.in/news/india/2020/10/29/china-among-largest-recipients-of-indias-covid-aid-reveals-rti-reply.html

Modi, N. (2020). PM's Address in ECOSOC commemoration of UN's 75th Anniversary. https://mea.gov.in/Speeches-Statements.htm?dtl/32838/PMs_Address_in_ECOSOC_commemoration_of_UNs_75th_Anniversary

Modi, N. (2021). PM's address to the Workshop on "COVID-19 Management: Experience, Good Practices and Way Forward" with 10 Neighboring

Countries". https://www.pmindia.gov.in/en/news_updates/pm-at-virtual-meeting-of-regional-health-officials-and-experts/

Pattanaik S. S. COVID-19 Pandemic and India's Regional Diplomacy. *South Asian Survey*. 2021; 28(1): 92-110.

Pattanaik, S. S. (2018). *India's Aid policy: A Response to China's Belt and Road Initiative in South Asia*. Asia Trend, Asia Centre, Paris, 80-88.

Pattanaik, S. S. (2020). SAARC COVID-19 Fund: Calibrating a Regional Response to the Pandemic. Strategic Analysis, 44(3), 241-52.

Prasad, R. (2020). Coronavirus | 18 generic drug companies pledge to make COVID-19 drugs for developing countries. *The Hindu*. https://www.thehindu.com/sci-tech/health/18-generic-drug-companies-pledge-to-make-covid-19-drug

Press Information Bureau (PIB). (2010). Ministry of Science and Technology, *Press Release*, https://pib.gov.in/PressReleasePage.aspx?PRID=1658123

Prime Minister's Office. (2021). Press Release. https://www.pmo.gov.bt/press-release-january-20-2021/

PTI. (2014). PTI, Times of India, (2014). *Maldives hit by Water Crisis, India Sends Help*. http://timesofindia.indiatimes.com/articleshow/45385033.cms?utm_source=contentofinterest&utm_medium=text&utm_campaign=cppst

Reserve Bank of India (2015). *Press Release*. https://www.rbi.org.in/scripts/BS_PressReleaseDisplay.aspx?prid=33544

Rubinhoff, A. G. (2000). The Multilateral Implications of Ethno-nationalist Violence in South Asia. *South Asian Survey*, 7(2), July-December, 273-293.

SAARC-COINEX. (2020). *About SAARC-COINEX*. https://saarc-coinex.org/saarc/aboutsaarccoinex

Sahay, A. (2020). "India can become the pharmacy of the world", *Business line*, https://www.thehindubusinessline.com/opinion/india-can-become-the-pharmacy-of-the-world/article31516558.ece

Sheriff, M. K. (2020). Eye on joint clinical trials, India training nations in South Asia. *Financial Express*. https://indianexpress.com/article/india/coronavirus-eye-on-joint-clinical-trials-india-training-nations-in-south-asia-7033839/

Shringla, H. V. (2020a). Foreign Secretary's virtual address to MIT World Peace University, Pune on the Importance of Multilateralism in the Time of a Global Pandemic—An Indian Perspective. https://mea.gov.in/Speeches-Statements.htm?dtl/32683/Foreign_Secretarys_virtual_address_to_MIT_World_Peace_University_Pune_on_the_Importance_of_Multilateralism_in_the_Time_of_a_Global_Pandemic__an_Indian

Shringla, H. V. (2020b). Foreign Secretary's virtual address to the National Defence College on 'India's Foreign Policy Options in the Emerging World Order'. https://mea.gov.in/SpeechesStatements.htm?dtl/32694/Foreign+Secretarys+virtual+addr

ess+to+the+National+Defence+College+on+Indias+Foreign+Policy+Options+in+the+Emerging+World+Order+May+15+2020

The Wire. (2020). Pakistan Joins Neighbours in Welcoming Modi's Call for SAARC to Combat COVID-19.

World Bank. (2020). *The Cursed Blessing of Public Banks.*

CHAPTER 5

Double Whammy: Managing Chinese Belligerence during COVID-19

India's COVID-19 Diplomacy: Factoring the 'China' Dynamics
While a debilitating pandemic rages on and countries all over the world have just one priority- to contain the rapid spread of the virus. However, it is important to look at important issues that have manifested themselves in India-China relations.

India has so far has been flat-footed in handling the challenges emerging from the pandemic domestically as well as through international diplomacy. Domestically, India acted swiftly to enforce a nation-wide lockdown. Regionally, it has led from the front in reviving SAARC's framework for creating a common fund pool specifically for the COVID-19 outbreak. Besides, it has sent medical teams, assistance and supplies to regional and extra-regional countries like Maldives, Sri Lanka, Nepal, Bangladesh, Bhutan, Kuwait, China, Brazil and the US. India's timely medical assistance to Brazil has pushed other countries of LAC region like Argentina, Chile, Ecuador, El Salvador to reach out to India for help.

Among great powers, India has kept a fine balance between China and the US. If the Indian Foreign Minister spoke with his counterparts in the US, UK and Australia, he equally engaged Russia and China. India's balanced approach between great powers, especially China and the US which are at loggerheads even amidst the pandemic, is further evident by its assistance to and cooperation with both China and the

US. While India has provided 15 tonnes of medical supplies to China comprising masks, gloves and other emergency medical equipment, India has cleared export of hydroxychloroquine (HCQ) to the US. The US has appreciated India's decision to provide wheat to Afghanistan during the ongoing crisis. In the immediate aftermath of India's decision to supply HCQ to the US, the US Department of State cleared Indian request to supply 16 MK 54 lightweight torpedoes and ten Harpoon Block II air-launched missiles for its latest maritime patrol aircraft. From China, India will soon be receiving 15 million PPE kits. However, India has sought to increase domestic production and lessen reliance on international imports after at least 50, 000 kits from China have failed India safety tests. So far, India has received 6,50,000 coronavirus testing kits from China. For instance, India is investing $1.3 billion to cut dependence on Chinese APIs. India is also looking at procuring medical equipment including testing kits from South Korea, the UK, the US, France, Japan, Malaysia and Germany.

China engaged in an early diplomacy with India after the US President Donald Trump labelled the coronavirus as "Chinese Virus". In a call between External Affairs Minister S. Jaishankar and his Chinese counterpart Wang Yi, India showed agreement with China that the virus should not be labelled. However, India has not shied away from mentioning COVID-19 in its official statement marking 45th anniversary of entry into force of the Biological and Toxin Weapons Convention (BWC). The statement calls for institutional strengthening of the Convention as well as the WHO and has asked states parties to the BWC "to recommit themselves to full and effective implementation of the Convention and full compliance with it, in letter and spirit".

However, India's engagement of China is not without its subterranean notions of friction. Officials in the Chinese Embassy of Delhi have come out strongly in criticism of news reports in the Indian media about labelling the virus as "Chinese virus". Besides, they have also criticised India media over media reports endorsing Taiwan's inclusion in the WHO. Calming nerves, the Indian envoy in Beijing, Vikram Misri, led from the front in advocating cooperation between India and China to develop a vaccine for the virus. China and India can cooperate on scientific and medical research side in the health and epidemiological sector as well as it will be useful for scientists and institutes of virology from both the countries to be in touch with each other.

Some of India's concerns emerge from the apprehension that Chinese entities' will take advantage of the crisis—and China's own seeming early recovery from the pandemic—for various objectives:

(1) the acquisition of vulnerable Indian companies,
(2) increasing its influence in India's neighbourhood, and
(3) portraying its system and global and regional leadership role as more effective than others (including the US and India)

Acting on these concerns, the Indian government revised its FDI policy impacting Chinese investments in India. Broadly, India's government has announced restrictions on foreign direct investment from countries that share a land boundary with India. It has also been proactive in its neighborhood with diplomatic outreach, economic aid, technical assistance, and the provision of medical supplies. Delhi's ability to respond to the competition for influence and over political systems will depend on how India ultimately fares in this crisis, in health, economic, and social terms. Meanwhile, India's leaders have been very active in engaging their counterparts around the world.

China is likely to closely watch what ensues after the promise of "coordinated effort" by India and the US in the Indo-Pacific domain. S Jaishankar and US Secretary of State Mike Pompeo have spoken over phone to discuss a joint strategy by India and the US to respond to the COVID-19 pandemic. This talk has been followed up by India's participation, led by Foreign Secretary Harsh V Shringla, in a telephonic conversation initiated by the US Deputy Secretary of State Stephen Biegun to discuss a common strategy and share best practices between countries of the Indo-Pacific region. The discussion included representatives from Australia, the Republic of Korea, Vietnam, New Zealand, and Japan with a pledge to continue the discussions on a weekly basis. The framework behind this weekly meeting is being called the 'Quad Plus' which also overlaps with the ASEAN+6 model. Although the success of this group is facilitating a regional strategy to deal with the COVID-19 outbreak remains to be seen, China will be keenly watching the developments and discussions between the Indo-Pacific countries. For India, which has been traditionally cautious about its role in the Quad, a more inclusive model like the "Quad Plus" could provide the necessary operational bandwidth in the region to move ahead with its Indo-Pacific vision. Moreover, with the US and its allies like Japan and Australia increasingly targeting China for the outbreak of COVID-19, there is a possibility of India being cornered in the Quad mechanism. As such, the "Quad Plus" framework is likely to suit India's position better in the current situation. Although India is unlikely to join other countries in asking for investigations into the origin of the Sars-Cov-2 virus, it is facing strong back channel pressure especially from the US and Australia. This could potentially shrink the bandwidth for strategic hedging between the US and China in the post COVID-19 world order. Prime Minister Modi had avoided participation in the Non-Aligned Movement for a few years now. But his most recent participation suggests that India is unlikely to stand with any one group of countries, despite gathering views that Indian is no longer a non-aligned country.

China's handling of the coronavirus pandemic has reinforced the skeptical perception of the country that prevails in many quarters in India. Some important China-hand in India like former Ambassador to China, Gautam Bambawale have said that China's image across most of the world has been dealt a serious blow as a result of the emotions amongst civil society and her hard power may be intact but her soft power has gone into negative territory. He has also said that the UN and its specialised agencies like the WHO have shown lack in direction, intent and effectiveness to tackle the pandemic.

The Indian state's rhetoric has been quite measured, reflecting its need to procure medical supplies from China and its desire to keep the relationship stable. Nonetheless, Beijing's approach has fueled Delhi's existing strategic and economic concerns.

Indian Pandemic Diplomacy South Asia
Among India's concerns is how China is using this crisis to expand its political presence in large parts of the globe, including in South Asia. South Asia has for long witnessed a see-saw diplomatic battle between India and China, but COVID-19 is adding fresh dimensions to this engagement. Especially, warming China-Nepal relations has been a concern for New Delhi. In particular, China has been ambitiously trying to influence politics in Kathmandu. After the first state visit of Xi Jinping to Nepal in October 2019, Chinese ambassador to Nepal Hou Yanqi tried to broker peace between recalcitrant factions of the ruling Nepal Communist Party (NCP) in the first week of May 2020. Yanqi held meetings with Oli, along with former Nepali PMs Pushpa

Kamal Dahal and Madhav Kumar Nepal. These developments have been watched closely by India.

India also launched a series of diplomacy in the Indian Ocean, helping countries of the Indian Ocean Region (IOR). India's assistance to other countries, especially in the Indian Ocean Region (IOR), amid the pandemic is being undertaken with the intention of further cementing its regional leadership. For instance, in Bangladesh, India scrambled to deliver medical supplies just before China. India has taken a host of initiatives in the region in cooperation and evacuation from Gulf countries to the small IOR nations.

Given China's continued aggression in the maritime domain despite the pandemic, particularly in the South China Sea, India is also keeping a close watch on China's activities in the maritime domain of the Indo-Pacific. Its deployment of a fleet of underwater drones in the Indian Ocean which collected more than 3,400 observations has made New Delhi more vigilant.

Starting the second week of April 2020, India began sending consignments of assistance of life-saving drugs to neighbouring countries to help them fight the coronavirus pandemic. Among countries in India's immediate and extended neighbourhood India sent drugs to Bhutan, Bangladesh, Afghanistan, Nepal, Myanmar, Seychelles, Mauritius and some African countries. Some countries such as Maldives, Seychelles and Mauritius are completely dependent on the Indian industry for supplies.

The COVID-19 pandemic proved once again that India's neighbourhood diplomacy is based on an agenda of friendship. It has proved to be an opportunity for India to also step up its neighbourhood diplomacy. On April 22, India sent 23 tonnes of essential medicines to Nepal to help it fight the coronavirus pandemic. This consignment included 8.25 lakh doses of essential medicines, 3.2 lakh doses of paracetamol and 2.5 lakh doses of HCQ. India's gesture was personally acknowledged with gratitude by the Prime Minister of Nepal K.P. Sharma Oli. In Bangladesh, India had already delivered 30,000 surgical masks and 15,000 head covers to Bangladesh by March 25. India followed this by gifting 1 lakh anti-malarial tablets of HCQ and 50,000 surgical gloves to Bangladesh, even as cases rose in that country. While in Maldives India supplied 317 cartons weighing over 5.5 tonnes of essential medicines, India has made medical supplies to Bhutan consisting of surgical masks, shoe covers, hand disinfectant/ hand sanitizers, digital thermometers, forehead sensor, disposable gloves, disposable surgical caps, surgical hoods, Gowns, fumigation systems, Glycerin, Glutaraldehyde solution , coveralls, safety goggles and medicines. India has also sent drugs to, Afghanistan, Myanmar, Seychelles, Mauritius and Sri Lanka where a plane with 10 tonnes of medicine was dispatched. India has sent rapid response teams to Afghanistan, Bangladesh, Bhutan, Maldives and Sri Lanka. For instance, in Maldives, a 14-member rapid response team was sent to help set up laboratories and a 15 member team comprising health care personnel from the Army was sent to Kuwait. Moreover, the Indian Air Force fleet were activated in the beginning of April to transport essential equipment and medicines and at least two warships have been kept on standby for quick deployment in India's immediate and extended neighbourhood. These steps are on the back of a SAARC level initiative started by PM Modi to reach out to all regional nations and creating a SAARC fund of $10 million to be used by the member states. The SAARC emergency fund has pledged a sum of $21.8 million with contributions from seven member countries. All SAARC nations except Pakistan have scrambled to fulfil their pledge to the emergency fund, with India already having delivered relief material worth $1.7 million to member states.

It was also decided that the Indian Army would ready rapid response teams to Sri Lanka, Bangladesh, Bhutan and Afghanistan, on the lines of the medical team it sent to the Maldives early in the outbreak. These teams are expected "to help boost (their) capabilities" in dealing with the ongoing health crisis. However, the move has been stalled since there was some apprehension in neighbouring countries about 'Army teams', particularly Sri Lanka and Nepal,

India produces more than 70 per cent of the world's HCQs. India has already sent 28 lakh HCQ and 13 lakh paracetamol tablets to 32 countries as assistance. In addition, drug supplies are being made to 42 countries on a commercial basis. For instance, while 530 kg of HCQ to Brazil has already been cleared by India, an additional 5 million tablets of HCQ has been offered to Brazil on a commercial basis.

To boost its own image—and perceptions of its reliability, in case countries and companies diversify more post-COVID-19—India lifted or made exceptions to its export restrictions on certain drugs. Indian officials have highlighted Delhi's assistance to China, and, while acknowledging Beijing's facilitation, emphasized that most of the supplies India is getting from China are commercially procured. Besides, India is engaging with other countries in the Indo-Pacific, bilaterally and through a Quad-plus mechanism. It will also likely work with others to blunt or balance China's future influence in institutions like the World Health Organisation.

China's Potential Loss is being seen as an Economic Opportunity for India

China's economy contracted for the first time in around three decades in the first quarter of 2020. In China, the greatest economic impact due to the pandemic has been on manufacturing and supply lines, and consequentially demand. Domestic restrictions have affected the supply chains of big companies such as industrial equipment manufacturer JCB and carmaker Nissan. Chinese car sales dropped by 86 percent in February 2020. The other source of major economic impact on Chinese economy will be in the form of global firms deciding to either scale down production or move out. In the economic realm, China has proved to be a component 'choke point' with stalled supplies to the world. Today, China accounts for close to 30 percent of global manufacturing, leading to manufacturing and supply chain clusters. The post-pandemic world will likely see attempts by countries to de-cluster by diversifying manufacturing and supply chains from China to other parts of the world. Already, Apple, Google and Microsoft have looked to move some hardware production from China to places including Vietnam and Thailand. Japan has led from the front in this regard by allocating $2.2 billion of its record economic stimulus package to help its manufacturers shift production out of China as the coronavirus disrupts supply chains between the major trading partners.

These developments have led to the debate whether India can provide an alternative to China in becoming a manufacturing base for firms pulling out from China. In this direction, India has offered land twice Luxembourg's size to firms leaving China. A total area of 461,589 hectares has been identified across the country for the purpose. The government has hand-picked 10 sectors—electrical, pharmaceuticals, medical devices, electronics, heavy engineering, solar equipment, food processing, chemicals and textiles—as focus areas for promoting manufacturing. It has asked embassies abroad to identify companies scouting for options. Invest India, the government's investment agency, has received inquiries mainly from Japan, the

US, South Korea and China, expressing interest in relocating to India.

Global Issues

WHO Reform

Although India has been silent on the US President Trump's move to cut WHO funding, it wants that the global body be reformed. During a virtual meeting of G20 leaders on March 26, Modi had called for the reform of inter-governmental organisations such as WHO, saying they were based on the last century's model and haven't adapted to deal with new challenges. There is increasing perception that UN reflects the world of 1945 and not that of 2020 and that it should be reformed, especially in the aftermath of the pandemic. Australia has supported India's call for the reform of the World Health Organisation (WHO) once the world has overcome the Coronavirus crisis as part of efforts to shape the post COVID-19 global order. India has also raised the issue of reform in the BRICS and Non-Aligned Movement forums.

Broadly, the China experts in India are of the opinion that the fissures between the United States on the one hand and China on the other have grown immeasurably as a result of this pandemic. Their battle for supremacy will continue. However, the issues and problems domestically within the United States have also become more apparent during this public health crisis. So while the US will continue to treat China as a peer competitor, it will also increasingly turn inward to resolve some of her own internal issues. This is a trend which existed before the political trends of the Wuhan virus but will accelerate now. On the other hand, with China's credibility being hurt badly, Beijing too has lost the moral authority to lead the world. As such, India sees this as a space for a group of middle powers to provide global leadership particularly on subjects which impact the whole of humanity. Perhaps, Japan, India, France, South Africa could form some type of coalition to lead the world towards measured outcomes. Needless to add, we would need to take both the United States and China along.

India-China relationship has always been very complex. Post pandemic, it has become more so. Both sides must remain calm but should be sensitive to each sides areas of concern. Globally, India could find some new diplomatic space to make its leadership felt on issues impacting humanity as a whole. It would be better for both countries to work together starting with Indian and Chinese scientists working together on developing a new vaccine against the novel corona virus. This could become a new sphere in which we could cooperate.

India's Policy overhaul Against China?

A recently conducted study by a former diplomat to China has concluded the following regarding India's policy overall vis-à-vis China:

> Recent developments have profoundly changed the outlook on the India-China relationship. For many decades, the prevailing framework was one where border and military disputes would be held in abeyance, while the countries concentrated on economic development and increased engagement. It is now clear that this framework must be discarded. What is less clear, however, is the new intellectual framework that must be adopted from the Indian perspective. The enumeration of policy choices, the development of a strategic perspective, and a carefully considered strategic framework, is the need of the hour in India.

While both sides continue to assert the importance of de-escalation, India has scrambled since last year to change its China policy over a period of time. These changes will be incremental in nature and will be spread over a period of time to avoid any shocks to the Indian economy. Among the immediate steps to be taken in 2020, while the standoff was still on, were lessening economic dependence on China. Behind the idea were: (1) reducing the trade deficit with China; (2) Finding alternative supply chains for imports and (3) reducing Chinese investments in India. These steps were meant to hurt China economically as India is a huge market for China. However, the impact of these steps haven't shown great results for two reason. First, these steps are long term in nature and immediate impact cannot be measured. Any abrupt snapping or reduction could lead to own economic shocks in India. Second, India's own economy in the pandemic surge has taken a dip and needs to be lifted up.

Economy

In the economic sector, India took certain steps in the year 2020 amidst the border standoff with China. India's trade with mainland China and Hong Kong declined by over 7 per cent to $109.76 billion in 2020, its steepest fall since 2013. It was a sharp reversal from the 3.2 per cent growth in trade in 2018-19 and the more robust 22 per cent jump in 2018. However, these dips were reversed in 2021 when China again climbed to becoming India's top trading partner.

Currently the government is looking at the following options suggested by a recent study with interest

There are three areas where there is a case for a retreat from engagement with China:

1. There is a case for introducing restrictions against companies controlled by the Chinese state from having a controlling stake in a hotlist of sensitive infrastructure assets (e.g. the JNPT or Delhi Airport though not (say) a highway from Nagpur to Nashik).
2. There is a need to avoid locking into Chinese-controlled technological standards and instead work with global standards processes. In particular, India must go on a path or mobile telephony, on questions such as 5G, with global standards and avoid Chinese- controlled standards.
3. India may police against and block Chinese state surveillance of Indian persons, which appears to often be done through backdoors in network equipment. Indian advocacy in international circles, of computer networks and technological standards where privacy is protected, would be more persuasive if the Indian state rises up to the checks and balances of healthy liberal democracies when it comes to state surveillance of citizens.

Relocating supply chains over a long period of time is also an important concern for India. In this regard, it is being suggested that alternative sourcing networks and destinations for Indian exports need to be systematically developed, to compensate for the adverse impact of these calibrated policy responses upon India-China engagement. The de-globalisation that is implied in these three paths—the reduced cross-border engagement for India with China—needs to be compensated by a strong path of opening up to the world economy so as to avoid the adverse impact upon India's growth possibilities through inward looking policies.

Of these three areas, in order to devise nuanced and calibrated responses as opposed to hurried sweeping decisions and bellicose headlines. Such decisions require deliberation, analysis and intellectual capacity in the policy process.

Considerations in the past:

1. The *Atmanirbhar Bharat* mission in India launched by PM Modi is intended to discourage imports from China and other countries while take large strides towards self-reliance.
2. Gradual reduction of Chinese companies from large infrastructure contracts.
3. The government has amended public procurement rules "to enable imposition of restrictions on bidders from countries which share a land border with India" on defence and national security grounds.
4. India's online procurement platform now requires vendors to identify the country of origin of products.
5. Lessening dependence on Chinese tankers to ship crude oil or petroleum products.
6. Close eye on rerouting of imports from China through third countries (consideration).

Additional Considerations

Cyber Security

India claims that state-sponsored Chinese hackers have repeatedly targeted its critical infrastructure, including power grids. The US-based cyber security firm found that a China-linked group called Red Echo was behind a surge in attacks on India's power infrastructure in 2020.

On October 12, 2020, the electricity went out in India's biggest city. Mumbai faced its worst power cut in decades, with businesses crippled, the stock market shut down, thousands of commuters stranded, and hospitals scrambling to ensure backup supply for their COVID-19 patients. Indian officials revealed in March 2021 that they might have found the cause of the power cut: a foreign cyber attack that targeted the servers of state power companies. Chinese hackers were the primary suspects. This is led the government to scramble to strengthen its cyber policies and defences, especially vis-à-vis China.

Cyber-crime has emerged as an important dimension of the India-China relationship. China is one of the countries which have created cyber crime and cyber warfare capabilities, which are termed 'advanced persistent threats' in the field of computer security. India is exposed to this problem from two points of view. First, there is the danger of attacks by state actors upon systems in India—government or private—as vehicles for inflicting harm upon India. Second, there are linkages between this problem and the greatest Indian export: software and processing services. Attacks upon systems built by Indian firms and attacks upon work being done in India for the global value chain of services production, could adversely impact India's most important industry. India thus has an interest in global solutions on cyber warfare and cyber crime.

Indian diplomacy needs to engage itself with like-minded countries, to build towards: (a) Frameworks for attribution through which attackers are identified through respected multilateral forums, thus avoiding the lack of trust in claims about attacks made by any one government; (b) A system of sanctions and adverse consequences imposed by multiple countries upon any attacker regardless of the identity of the victim; (c) Establishment of treaties with countries where governments agree to not attack each other; (d) Build towards international frameworks akin to the regime of nuclear control; and

(e) Placing the behaviour of Chinese state actors on these questions as one element of the diplomatic relationship with China.

Indo-Pacific

India embarked on a major foreign policy overdrive during the pandemic in 2020, bringing its vision for a rules-based Indo-Pacific as a cornerstone of its diplomacy and displaying a steely resolve to fashion a regional environment conducive to its strategic interests in the face of China's transgression attempts in eastern Ladakh that caused the most serious damage to the bilateral relations in over four decades. As the bitter border standoff with China forced it to recalibrate its external engagements, India mounted a diplomatic push, focusing on boosting ties with major global players like the US, Japan, the UK and France with a larger goal to increase its geo-political heft and position itself as a credible force wedded to peace, stability and international law in contrast to Chinese assertion.

Direct consequences of this policy revision:
1. Strengthening of the Quad
2. Enhanced net-security-provider role (assuming more regional responsibilities)
3. Increasing multilateral partnerships and expanding Quad's agenda.

The expansion of the Indo-Pacific agenda now focuses on three main aspects for India. Broad basing the agenda through a dual purpose—including more partners particularly the Quad Plus mechanism and by intensifying the group's activities such as more frequent exercises and full operationalisation of Logisitics and communications agreements with various countries.

1. Border Infrastructure

There are two main highways that connect Ladakh to the rest of India, but they are closed for at least four months every winter. The only way urgent supplies are sent to Ladakh during these months is by air. The government has identified 73 strategically important roads along the Chinese border, of which 61 are with the Border Roads Organisation (BRO), running over 3,300 km (2,000 miles). A parliamentary committee report in March noted that 75 per cent of the work under BRO had been completed.

India has sped up infrastructure near China border, even as the stand-off at LAC continued. Since 2020, the Defence Minister's office is directly keeping a tab of the progress of the infrastructure being built near the border with China with frequent high level meetings. In order to expedite the implementation of the road projects, the financial and administrative powers of BRO executives have been enhanced. On March 15, Defence minister Rajnath Singh speaking in the Upper House said that said in Rajya Sabha that connectivity on 59 critical roads has been achieved along the India-China border. The minister, in a written response to a question, said as many as 61 India-China Border Roads (ICBRs) with a length of 3,323.57 km were identified as strategically important. The work was entrusted to the Border Roads Organisation (BRO). The construction of 42 roads with a length of 1,530.38 km has been completed. On 59 roads of 3,205.16 km in length, connectivity has already been achieved. While on the remaining two roads of 118.41 km length, the unconnected portion is 29 km.

By March 2021, 10 more ICBR roads have been completed. While development work on seven roads is likely to be over by the month of March in 2021 and work on another two roads is expected to be over by March 2023. 61 roads, 27 roads with a length of 1,725.46 km are in the state of Arunachal Pradesh, 12 roads with a length of 1,064.14 km are in Ladakh and 14 roads with a length of 355 km are in the state of Uttarakhand. Also, there are five ICBR roads in Himachal Pradesh of length 116.99 km, while the state of Sikkim has three roads with a length of 61.98 km.

Besides the aforementioned, the Indian government has pushed 6 new road projects in Arunachal as tension with China continues. The length of 6 stretches is 100 km and work is expected to take 2 years to complete. For the first time, National Highways Infrastructure Development Corporation (NHIDCL), under roads ministry, has got the projects instead of BRO, under defence ministry. This is done to expedite the work near the border. As of now, soldiers walk on foot for three to four days to reach some of the forward locations on this road. Once the roads are built, it will take about 7-10 hours.

Besides the roads being built in Arunachal Pradesh, NHIDCL has also been handed projects to build at least six tunnels to improve connectivity to Ladakh and Jammu and Kashmir. The most crucial among these is the 13.5 km tunnel at Shinkhun La pass in Himachal Pradesh, which will provide an alternate route to Leh. At present one has to go through Zojila in Kashmir to reach Leh. The road is closed during the winter months because of snow. Five more tunnels are also coming up in J&K. This includes the Zojila and Z-Morh tunnel, the 12 km-long Daranga tunnel at Shudh Mahadev, which will provide an alternate route to Srinagar via Anant Nag, and the 10 km Vailoo tunnel at Sinthan Pass.

Reliance on Continued Cooperation with China but with caution and gradual retaliation

Continued cooperation with China with caution is going to be the way forward. This will include increased vigil at the border interspersed with CBMs; Removing misperceptions; strengthening commitments in the Indo-Pacific through robust international partnerships (building favorable coalitions). The part of removing misperceptions has included India's effort to understand China better, to be able to frame better policies vis-à-vis China.

India is going to continue to delicately push further the investigations regarding the COVID-19 pandemic, without naming China as the responsible country for the outbreak. India has officially responded to the recently released WHO-convened global study on the origin of COVID-19. In this regard, India has said that, "It is pertinent to note that the Director General of the WHO has separately raised the issue of delays and difficulties in accessing raw data for the team conducting the study.... We join other stakeholders in voicing their expectations that follow up to the WHO Report or further studies, including on an understanding of the earliest human cases and clusters by the WHO on this critical issue, will receive the fullest cooperation of all concerned. We share the need for a comprehensive and expert-led mechanism that would expeditiously investigate the origin of COVID-19 in cooperation with all stakeholders." While China has dodged a call for further probe into the origins of the virus.

The government has also doled out a scheme to allocate Rs. 10,000 crore to boost the production of APIs (Active Pharmaceutical Ingredients) in India in conjunction with a plan to increase trade barriers and tariffs on around 300 imported items. These include many items imported from China. China has already raised concerns on India's raised tariff at the WTO.

Eye on Indirect Elements of War

The indirect-war elements are conspicuous in China's actions against India. China has steadily brought Indian security under pressure through unconventional instruments, including cyberattacks, its reengineering of the cross-border flows of rivers, and its nibbling away at disputed Himalayan territories. In the disputed Himalayan borderlands, China has mixed conventional and unrestricted tactics. For example, China has set out to quietly build some 624 villages in the region.

China's non-recognition of Ladakh as India's part is likely to see a graded response from India in which India will loosely hold to the principles of One-China policy. This policy has started with signalling on Taiwan issue. From appointing a leading diplomat to its front organization in Taiwan and two BJP members attending the Taiwanese President's swearing in, India's MEA has for the first time expressed its official message to Taiwan's tragic train wreck.

Continued unreliability on China coupled with military preparation and Coalition Building

As India and China negotiate a complex disengagement process to pull back their troops and weapons from friction points in eastern Ladakh, the air forces of both countries remain to be deployed in the theatre just as they were when the border row was at its peak last year. By taking military action in 2020, China has clearly indicated that she does not desire a stable, balanced, forward looking relationship with India and that she is willing to use military coercion to resolve her disputes with India. It is felt in India that all earlier bilateral agreements aimed at maintaining peace and tranquility in the India-China border areas have been violated by China.

In military affairs, China is substantially ahead of India on the agenda of modernising the armed forces, of reducing the head count and increasing the technological intensity behind each soldier. There is a need to fundamentally reorient Indian military spending away from the predominance of wages and pensions towards right sized armed forces who have more modern capabilities, where the share of wages and pensions in overall military expenditure comes down to below half.

With the region witnessing new geopolitical alignments, India too redoubled efforts to boost strategic cooperation with countries in India's immediate neighbourhood, Gulf region, Central Asia and member nations of the ASEAN (Association of Southeast Asian Nations) grouping. In the same spirit, India is building stronger regional bonds in South Asia. Keeping its neighbourhood policy intact in the face of growing competition in neighbouring countries such as Sri Lanka, Maldives, Myamar etc. is a priority for the Indian government right now. India has luached its Vaccine Maitri initiative to provide vaccines free of cost and through commercial channels to its neighbours.

As such the recent study on China has suggested the following regarding India's policy.

The India-China relationship is much more than the problem of mobilising troops in Ladakh in 2021. It is a long-term game. It is not just about military affairs; it is about economics, science, technology, etc. It is a unique situation where diplomacy must come to the fore. In the short run, the hand of cards which India has been dealt is not favourable. Indian economic and military power cannot be easily changed in the short run. In the short run, containing China will require forming coalitions of like-minded countries, a path that is new for Indian foreign policy. Alongside this, a long-run strategy must simultaneously be put into motion. In many ways, India is better placed to establish a dynamic market economy located in a liberal democracy, as compared with Xi Jinping's China.

In the short run, India will fare best through participating in coalitions to balance China. These coalitions would naturally consist of countries with shared values and interests. As an example, once an appropriate deep trade agreement is in place, the natural focus of finance and trade for Sri Lanka or Bangladesh is with India and after that, their interests would lie in supporting a strong and successful India. Three groups of countries are our natural partners in such coalition building: (a) the major democracies of the world, (b) the countries in the Indian region and (c) countries that share a border with China, including major powers such as Russia, who are our natural partners in this venture. Building such coalitions including the Quad and others is the need of the hour.

India's China Policy

India's China policy has been in the want of a long-term strategy to deal with China. Until now, India's China policy was guided by a piecemeal and issue-based approach. However, the discussions over the recent border standoff with China has underscored the need for policy reformulations in dealing with China. Although, much of this remain unstated in the popular media. It is hard to tell whether there is a concrete strategy to from a China-policy from New Delhi at this stage but some indications point out the main priorities of the Government in New Delhi in dealing with China differently than in the past. This broad strategy has four dimensions:

1. Lessening Economic Dependence on China; narrowing the trade deficit with China and limiting Chinese investments in India to the extent possible. This also includes the readiness to hurt China economically in times of crises, like it was evinced amidst the ongoing border crisis at the LAC.

2. Framing a peace-time border policy to avoid repeat of border clashes with China and ensure that the status quo is maintained until a strong bilaterally agreed framework is agreed upon. This includes upping the ante on border infrastructure along the border with China at unprecedented pace through the Border Roads Organisation (BRO).
3. Increasing its Indo-Pacific resolve through building capacities, partnerships at the multilateral and assuming more responsibilities in the region towards boosting its net-security provider role in the Indo-Pacific.
4. Ensuring cooperation with China continues at the bilateral and multilateral levels to avoid any sudden jerks for the economy.

I. Lessening Dependence

The concept of raising the costs is often used in Indian defence discourse. It means that India should inflict incremental damage on Pakistan every time when the latter attacks India either overtly or covertly. This thought, however, is beginning to gain grounds vis-à-vis China in three domains– diplomatic, strategic and economic. Of course such a strategy would not be immediate in the case of China and would depend on India's ability to inflict such costs with a country with which it has huge trade deficit (of US$ 56.77 billion in 2019).

A recent study has suggested that India has the potential to reduce the trade deficit by $8.4 billion over the next financial year (FY22) through rationalisation of a part of the imports on selected 40 categories in which India already has available manufacturing facility/infrastructure, and it is in addition to this that we need to work on several fronts.

Steps against China

Demand for stringent economic measures against China is most vocal in this crisis. It is necessary to consider different aspects of this issue in order to know the extent of measures required. There is growing call for boycotting of Chinese products and uninstalling Chinese apps from mobile phones. There has also been an effort to reduce India's dependence on Chinese goods. The Indian Railways, for instance, cancelled an INR 471 crore deal with a Chinese firm. Similarly, state-owned telecom firm BSNL was instructed not to use gear from Chinese firm Huawei for a network upgrade. The government has mandated all products to have the Country of Origin tag for products on the Government e-Marketplace in an effort to identify Chinese-origin goods. In early July 2020, the Ministry of Power restricted power supply systems and networks import from China citing cyber and security threats, which constitute about 30 per cent of the total imports from China. In the last 10 years, 12,540 MW out of 22,420 MW of the super critical power plants were built using Chinese equipment. India also extended safeguard taxes on imports of solar cells and modules as well as imposed anti-dumping duty on several goods. In July, India placed colour television sets imports under the restricted category, thus requiring a licence to import; and air conditioners under the prohibited category. The effects of these moves cannot be measured immediately.

The highly complex nature and interconnectedness of the globalised world means this step would require long time to materialise. China is the second largest trading partner of India after the US. But India has a trade deficit with China. India-China trade was more than US$ 84 billion in 2019 of which India's exports to China were just US$ 16 billion while imports from China were more than US$ 68 billion. At the time when there are calls to ban China's imports, India needs to create an alternate arrangement either through incentivising domestic production or substituting imports from China with imports from any other country. Along with India, China is also a major trade partner of the US and Russia and has large investments in both these countries.

It will be a challenge since Indian pharmaceutical and automobile companies depend a great deal on imports from China. Increasing of duties on imports and boycotting Chinese products is only a part of the solution. In April the central government changed FDI rules. According to new rule, any country that shares land border with India would require central government's permission to invest in India. This rule would curtail China's future investments. But China already has substantial investments in India. China has invested heavily in start-ups in India. China has invested in 18 out of 30 start-ups in India. China's investment in Indian start-ups is more than US$ 4 billion. Along with the new FDI rules, government needs to take steps to get Indian investors to invest in the start ups.

At the height of the border conflict with China, India had decided that imports from China would be limited. However, that strategy has hit India tools China is its largest trade partner with a huge trade deficit in favour of China. Therefore, it has been thought to be wise to do away with abrupt breaks in trade with China and instead deal with lessening trade dependence on China over long term as a strategy. As such, China is back as India's number one trading partner for 2020. The Modi government is also set to clear Chinese FDI projects worth US$ 2 billion in India. The bilateral trade that stood at US$ 3 billion in the year 2000 grew to US$ 92.68 billion in 2019. China was India's second-largest trading partner in 2019 and emerged as the largest trading partner in the first half of FY 20-21. As such,

China forms an integral part of the global supply chain, and India too is heavily dependent on Chinese imports, ranging from a variety of raw materials to critical components.

II. Increased Vigil despite De-escalation

After more than a year of being on the verge of a war in eastern Ladakh, mutual disengagement by Indian and Chinese forces from north and south bank of Pangong Tso was completed with clockwork military precision duly between 10 and 19 February and the whole process was recorded in video for posterity. However, this seems to be the first phase of a likely comprehensive agreement between India and China to restore status quo ante April 2020 at the Line of Actual Control (LAC). No progress has been made with respect to disengagement from Depsang Plains, Hot Springs-Gogra, and Demchok at the 10th Corps Commander-level meeting held on 20 February. Troops remain in a face-off situation in these areas.

Disengagement of frontline troops in the Pangong Tso area was a significant step forward for resolution of other areas in the Western Sector, India and China at the 10th Corps Commander talks agreed to push for a mutually acceptable solution of remaining issues.

The 21st meeting of the Working Mechanism for Consultation and Coordination on India-China Border Affairs (WMCC) was held on 12 March and it reiterated the commitment of both sides to continue negotiations for disengagement from remaining areas. It was also agreed that the 11th Corps Commander-level meeting would be scheduled soon.

There is a feeling that India relied too much on the sanctity of the four border agreements and frameworks that it signed with China in 1993 and that many of the core founding principles of the border agreements are being disregarded. This has called the CSG and other bodies to deal with China in a pragmatic way and keep up border vigils even during seemingly peaceful times.

Most recently, India is keenly watching the Chinese People's Conference formally approved mega hydro projects on lower reaches of Yarlung Zangbo River (Brahmaputra) and US$ 30 billion infrastructure projects in Tibet, several of them close to our Himalayan borders.

III. Focus on Indo-Pacific along with other partners

Along with strengthening land border security, India needs equal focus on the maritime domain as well. Clashes at the border are only a part of China's actions against India. India also needs a concrete plan to protect its interests in the maritime domain. India could do this at individual level or by expediting strategic cooperation with countries like the US, Japan, Australia, Vietnam and even Russia. Interestingly, of the three branches of military—Army, Navy and Air Force—Navy is the only branch that has a written maritime doctrine. This document defines the areas of primary and secondary interests for the Navy in the maritime domain. India could also think about publishing a defence white paper which would define India's defence interests and policies in a comprehensive and collective manner.

India has in general stayed away from taking a defined stand on the contested power politics and maintained cordial relations with most of the stakeholders of this region by engaging bilaterally as well as within plurilateral and multilateral platforms with its Indo-Pacific partners. Inclusiveness, openness, ASEAN centrality have been the predominant pillars of India's conception of the Indo-Pacific. But given Chinese aggression along the Sino-Indian border, especially after the 15 June 2020 clash with PLA troops in the Galwan Valley in Ladakh, India is in the process of redefining its priorities in the wider

Indo-Pacific region even as it re-evaluates its assumptions underlying China policy. The choice to work closely with like-minded countries and develop a stronger stance against China's "not so peaceful rise" is viewed as a priority now by New Delhi. Like several other countries in the Indo-Pacific, India is also hardening its policy posture vis-à-vis China. In more ways than one, however, it is the rise of China that has been instrumental in shaping New Delhi's vision for a free and open Indo-Pacific. China's growing ambitions, its increasingly aggressive foreign policy posture, and its border skirmishes with New Delhi have evoked a disconcerting feeling, forcing India to focus its energies on the rise of Beijing and establish itself in a leading role in the Indo-Pacific.

The US as a Factor

Unlike in 2017, US support for India at a time of confrontation with China is much more pronounced during the border conflict with China. It remains to be seen what stand does the Biden administration take in case of a potential conflict or confrontation with China.

The consultations between the two sides are much more open, and the United States has publicly and repeatedly supported India. Even prior to the Galwan clash that resulted in the deaths of 20 Indian Army personnel, senior Indian and US officials appear to have been in contact. In one of the first conversations amid the border stand-off, Indian Defense Minister Rajnath Singh and US Secretary of Defense Mark T. Esper spoke on the phone on 29 May. The two sides discussed the state of bilateral defense ties and agreed to keep up with their efforts "for a strong and enduring U.S.-India defense partnership."

A virtual Quad summit was held by the leaders of the US, India, Japan and Australia on 12 March. The joint statement issued by the White House, and also published as an oped in The Washington Post, is indicative of a broad-based grouping for cooperation in the Indo-Pacific. China, though unnamed, was clearly the focus, but it was also indicative of the limitations of the Quad given each member's complex individual relationship with China.

The Quad Meeting and Lyon Austin's Visit to India

The US-Japan-India-Australia video Summit and the visit of the US Defense Secretary to India have made observers once again focus on India's positioning in the Indo-Pacific and even the global landscape. China's aggression and deeper India-US bilateral and multilateral cooperation was the focus of 20 March meeting between Defence Minister Rajnath Singh and the visiting US Secretary of Defense Lloyd Austin. The focus was to get to know each other and see how the defence and strategic cooperation can be carried forward amid continued aggression by China in the region and beyond. During the visit, both countries identified artificial intelligence, information sharing, logistics, space and cyber as key areas of cooperation besides expanding military-to-military engagement.

A large part of the reason why this Quad summit is extraordinary is that it uses "vaccine cooperation" as the fulcrum, focuses on the supply chain issues of the industrial chain, and clearly highlights the status of India as a potential manufacturing centre.

Lloyd Austin's Visit

Austin's visit came close on the heels of the first-ever Quad summit, during which Prime Minister Narendra Modi said the grouping had come of age and would remain an important pillar of stability in the region. The Indian Defence Minister hinted at increased combined activities in the Indo-Pacific through a full-realisation of the foundational agreements between the two countries. In this regard, he said that, "We reviewed the wide gamut of bilateral and multilateral exercises and agreed to pursue enhanced cooperation with the US Indo-Pacific Command, Central Command and Africa Command," he added. "Acknowledging that we have in place the foundational agreements, LEMOA, COMCASA and BECA, we discussed steps to be taken to realise their full potential for mutual benefit."

The reference to "the most pressing challenges" in the Indo-Pacific region is aimed at China's belligerence in the Indo-Pacific region and beyond. Modi's reference to democracy, and commitment to a rules-based order is also a veiled reference to Beijing.

"Both sides exchanged perspectives on shared challenges confronting the region and committed to further strengthen their broad ranging and robust defence cooperation," the US Embassy said after Mr. Austin's meetings with PM Modi and National Security Advisor Ajit Doval.

Indo-US cooperation on defence and intelligence has been of very high quality in the last 10 months, and involved sharing of high-end satellite images, telephone intercepts, and data exchange on Chinese troops and weapon deployment along the Line of Actual Control. New Delhi has been watching Chinese movements in "all sectors" of the LAC, with some help from the US and its platforms. The Indian armed forces have used at least five American platforms at the LAC in eastern Ladakh—the C-17 Globemaster III for military transport, the Chinook CH-47 as heavy-lift helicopters, the Apache for threatening armour, the P-8I Poseidon for overland reconnaissance, and the C-130J for airlifting troops.

Other areas of India's focus in the Indo-Pacific with China in mind

Besides, India's Indo-Pacific is going to pivot itself on countries beyond just the Quad members. By emphasising on ASEAN-centrality, India is looking at the ASEAN+6 countries to enhance stakes on the eastern side of the Strait of Malacca. Three other countries in particular for India's focus are Vietnam, Indonesia and the Philippines.

Other important focus areas in the Indo-Pacific:
1. Focus on the Bay of Bengal
2. Focus on Western Indian Ocean
3. Full-scale use and implementation of Logistics agreements with the US, France and Singapore realise the true potential of net-security-provider
4. Extending inland maritime connectivity to the Bay of Bengal for improving connectivity with Myanmar and Bangladesh
5. Focus on SAGAR Doctrine to improve regional connectivity
6. Emphasis on the Indo-Pacific oceans Initiative (IPOI) as India's brand of outlook in the region. Using this Initiative, India plans to support the building of a rules-based regional architecture resting on seven pillars. These are: maritime security; maritime ecology; maritime resources; capacity building and resource sharing; disaster risk reduction and management; science, technology and academic cooperation & trade connectivity and maritime transport. I am happy to note that today's workshop is focussing on two of the pillars namely maritime security and connectivity.

Reliance on Continued Cooperation with China but with caution

So far, India, in its quest for multilateralism, has been careful either not to name China or project itself as countering interests of China. India has maintained, especially with reference to Indo-Pacific, that interests of all the powers must be protected. However, there is a realisation that China cannot be countered by a disconnected approach. It implies India's accommodative approach against China's aggression is a mismatch. India needs to be more vocal about China's actions that harm India not just at the border but also at regional and international level. Most recently, India and China held bilateral consultations on UNSC issues today using the VTC platform.

Conclusion

There is a feeling that many of the core founding principles of the border agreements are being disregarded. India-China relationship stands evolved after the border conflict. India and China will have a different kind of trading partnership going forward, one where de-hyphenation of border conflict/resolution with other issues will be not so easy as in the past. The biggest obstacle to the boundary being resolved is the Chinese view that the boundary can be leveraged to some extent and settling it is giving something away to India that they can't use later. The Indian view is that settling the boundary should be a prerequisite to better relations.

Overall, the so-called "Wuhan spirit" did not have much of an impact in galvanising Sino-Indian ties in a positive direction. Furthermore, China's apprehension about India's aspirations to play a larger role in the regional and global arena remains strong. With the two nations jostling for influence in their respective neighbourhoods and beyond, the 2020 border crisis was the last straw for a fundamental reappraisal of India's China policy as well as its larger regional outlook. Managing the strategic challenge from China has become the topmost foreign policy priority for India. With growing concerns in India about China's expansionist tendencies, India is ready to embark on a more proactive role in the region, reflected in a range of policy choices New Delhi has made in recent times both about the region and China. Given Chinese sensitivities, India had been reluctant to brand its Indo-Pacific policy as a "strategy" but has mostly referred to it as its "vision" for the Indo-Pacific. As a more robust Quad takes shape and as other regional powers also recalibrate their China ties, India is trying to devise a stronger Indo-Pacific approach with other like-minded nations. The securitisation of the Quad with joint military exercises and moves toward greater interoperability might be the first step as a new security architecture emerges in the maritime geography.

In every aspect ranging from trade and technology to regional and global collaborations, Indian foreign and security policy is being designed with the aim of tackling the China challenge.

The Road Ahead

Over the long-term, India may be considering the following four alternatives to lessen asymmetric economic dependence on China (there is some debate on these issues).

1. Import Substitution

By this, we do not only mean substituting non-essential imports with already manufactured alternatives or potentially easy ones to produce but also examine other items that can be imported from other countries at comparable prices. This can be an opportunity to strengthen trade relations with other countries and enable mutual benefits for the economies, thus, catalysing recovery from the COVID-19 crisis.

2. Attracting Investments

The corona virus pandemic has led to major corporations contemplating shifting their manufacturing bases from China. India can attract a few of them by implementing a competitive strategy that would require radical changes in law, particularly in the areas of land acquisition, labor issues, tax incentives, and ensuring quick permissions/clearances.

3. Empowering Local Substitutes
Many local goods fail to compete with their Chinese counterparts due to their incredibly low-cost or high-value for money. The government can help boost the demand for local substitutes by providing tax benefits, rate cuts to reduce costs, and incentives to improve quality. Using the expertise of institutes of eminence and those of national importance, an enabling ecosystem can be created for improving the quality and marketing of these products. The ODOP initiative of the government of UP could be a model to begin with.

4. Reciprocal Policies for Chinese firms
The government can make it mandatory for new Chinese entrants to have a joint venture with an Indian firm as a partner, should they choose to start a business in India (a similar policy is followed by China). Software companies should be urged to set up their data centres at Indian locations with necessary controls on data usage, access, and dissemination.

The 'second' wave of COVID-19 caught India off-guard. It began in mid-March 2021 and by the end of April, daily infections had rocketed to over 400,000. The tremendous challenge for India's government was too much to bear and that was clear in the statistics. The role of the civil society was really important in this phase. The China challenge during the pandemic scaled up India's challenges during the pandemic doubly. The Indian diplomacy faced an unprecedented challenge in the form of COVID-19. In many ways, the Indian politics, its domestic circumstances and international connections, all stood upended by the COVID-19 challenge. A new form of diplomacy had to be started, in the face of restrictions on physical mobility and the world's readjustments to the 'online' ways. Small and big powers, regional and global powers had to be engaged in the same measure, especially with different levels of access engendered by the pandemic and different levels of impact of the pandemic on various countries. India started engagements with a wide spectrum of countries including great powers, middle powers, smaller powers and its neighbors just when COVID-19 hit. The initial challenges posed at the beginning of the pandemic were enormous, mostly because of the scale of activities involved. The pandemic proved to be a test for India's external relations, as relations with other countries had to be translated into partnerships for enhanced and emergency requirements during the pandemic. It was a tremendous challenge for India's High Commissions and Embassies abroad.

www.ingramcontent.com/pod-product-compliance
Lightning Source LLC
Chambersburg PA
CBHW020414230426
43664CB00009B/1273